I0816742

MEGA RETURNS

MEGA RETURNS

PROFIT FROM MAXIMUM PESSIMISM

DAVID SKARICA

Humanix Books
MEGA RETURNS

Humanix Books, P.O. Box 20989, West Palm Beach, FL 33416, USA
www.humanixbooks.com | info@humanixbooks.com

ISBN: 978-1-63006-272-9 (Hardcover)
ISBN: 978-1-63006-273-6 (E-book)

Printed in the United States of America
10 9 8 7 6 5 4 3 2 1

This book is dedicated to Chris Crupi,
who passed away in 2020.
One of my best friends and business partners.
May he rest in peace.

Contents

Introduction

End of the Debt Super Cycle

I started to think about and write this book in 2019, prior to the outbreak of Covid-19, better known as the coronavirus, a pandemic that made an unprecedented impact on the global markets. The financial impact of a widespread pandemic is something the modern global economy has never witnessed before. While we know Covid-19 was a driving factor in the crash of 2020, it was also an excuse for the market to "sell off" and to "correct." We had an immense buildup of debt and speculation in the market, resulting in the entire market becoming a massive "bubble." When the market bubbles, or "tops out," as it did at the end of February, it obviously becomes extremely vulnerable to any external shocks. If the market had traded at "normal" valuations instead of near all-time high values, it might have only corrected, but instead it had a mini-crash. What is even scarier is now, as I write in 2025, valuations are back to extreme valuations. There are now bubbles in artificial intelligence and the Magnificent Seven.

We are coming to the end of an era: the era of asset price inflation and bubbles driven by a huge explosion in debt that has continually picked up steam and accelerated since the 2008 financial crisis. Since the United States got off the gold standard in 1971, we have seen an explosion of debt at all levels of the global economy. From government debt, consumer debt, investment corporate debt, junk corporate debt, student debt, to emerging market debt, the list goes on. When the global economy went pure fiat in 1971, it meant that nothing backed the fiat dollars and other currencies in circulation, so governments could de facto print as much money as they wanted to bail out the economy and create asset bubbles.

In the 1980s, there was a period of financial liberalization; Ronald Reagan, Margaret Thatcher, and other leaders deregulated financial markets. This, combined with a pure fiat system, became a perfect scenario for the financial markets. The financialization of New York and London, along with currencies that could be printed limitlessly, resulted in great prosperity in the financial and credit markets.

For the last 15 years, the explosion of debt and ease of money printing has caused global stock market and property market expansion. However, it has also left governments worldwide vulnerable to a large downturn in the economy. The result of these bailouts is grim; the impending downturn will inevitably bankrupt affluent Western nations and send shockwaves through second-tier economies.

I firmly believe we are nearing the endgame of this debt super cycle, and the Coronavirus Crash is the catalyst for the impending transition. Since 2009, we have seen a gross acceleration of the debt bubble. During the worst periods of the 2008 financial crisis, governments saw an explosion in deficit spending to keep economies afloat, and in many cases had to rack up enormous deficits to bail out the financial system. We again saw another surge in debt during the 2020–2021 coronavirus period to bail out the economy.

Take Canada, for example, a nation that had a debt-to-GDP ratio of about 70% before the 2008 financial crisis. Canada's debt-to-GDP ratio is now near 90%, and if you were to include the Canadian provinces, each of which have their own debt issues, the debt-to-GDP ratio is closer to 120%. Australia, which had one of the lowest debt-to-GDP ratios at only 16% before the financial crisis, has seen their ratio more than double to 40%. Similarly, Canada and Australia have private debt to GDP of over 150%, with the value in their respective property markets skyrocketing. Private-debt-to-GDP in Canada is at an astonishing 170%, as mortgage debt has exploded during the housing boom (and bubble) during the last 15 years. These offshoot bubbles, such as the property bubbles in Australia and Canada and corporate debt bubbles in the United States, are all based on low interest rates. This will have a major effect on the debt-driven portions of the economy, which have benefited from the debt cycle and cheap money. Therefore, if interest rates climb in a debt crisis, it will absolutely affect all parts of the economy.

Even the so-called creditor nations have seen debt expand to grow their economies. China has seen debt to GDP rise from 33% in 2007 to 77% currently. This does not consider the massive expansion of the Chinese banking system. By some estimates, the Chinese banking system is five times larger than the U.S. banking sector was at the height of the housing bubble!

The increase of debt is not unique to the government's deficit. In fact, a similar trend can be seen across many different sectors. Student loans in the United States, estimated at roughly $650 million before the financial crisis, have now surpassed a figure of $1.3 trillion! Furthermore, corporations have nearly tripled their debt in the last 20 years from $3 trillion to $12 trillion—a figure that comprises nearly 40 percent of GDP. Keep in mind, much of this corporate debt was incurred by funding buybacks and keeping the stock market bubble afloat.

The biggest issue with all these staggering numbers is very simple. The room for growth is limited. Before the current financial crisis, many governments had low debt-to-GDP levels after a near, 20-year global economic expansion. However, these debts accrued as governments ran huge deficits to keep economies afloat during the financial crisis. Subsequently, the failure to balance budgets and pay back debts during the time of economic upturn has led to an explosion of debt for many large corporations and governments alike.

Nowhere is this more apparent than in the United States, the global superpower and largest economy in the world, where nearly 10 years into an economic expansion, deficits were running over $1 trillion (nearly 5% of GDP prior to 2008). This failure to properly manage deficits in a time of economic prosperity leaves us in a position to increase our deficits to $3 trillion–$4 trillion, or nearly 15%–20% of GDP, as the government attempts to bail out the economy. Even now as I write in 2024, deficits are near $2 trillion, or 7% of GDP, during an economic expansion. The deficit for August 2024 alone was $380 billion, or north of 1% of GDP, for one month!

The danger is that there is no cushion for debt to continue to accrue in the future; there is a limit. The government will not be able to stimulate or absorb a downturn after another market crash on par with 2008. If there is any sort of return to the "bond vigilantes" (investors who will crush bonds and raise longer-term interest rates looking for larger returns or forcing governments to become financially solvent), then governments will be broken at every major international level.

The government bailed out the financial sector during the last two financial recessions, but who will bail out the government? I am primarily concerned with the impending scenario where superpowers such as China and the United States will need to be bailed out.

With the election of Trump and the Republicans taking the Senate and House, many think a huge boom is coming, but it should be noted that most of the large crashes in market history (1929, 1974, 1987, 2008) happened under Republican administrations when investors suffer from what Alan Greenspan referred to "irrational exuberance," as the booms tend to be greater (John Kenneth Galbraith also discussed this in his excellent book *A Short History of Financial Euphoria*).

Trump is no fiscal conservative. In 2019 pre-Covid, he was running a near $1 trillion deficit during an economic expansion. As we go to press, the deficit for fiscal 2024 is estimated near $2.3 trillion and the United States has the largest net deficit in the Organisation for Economic Co-operation and Development (OECD). The national debt is $36 trillion, or over 120% of GDP. Despite the Federal Reserve cutting interest rates in September 2024 by 50 basis points, long-term yields are moving higher, and I feel a major reason for this is worries over a debt crisis in the next few years.

The good news about a Trump administration is if there is a debt crisis, I think he would be more likely to cut spending and reform outlay programs that need to be overhauled. (I think a Harris administration would just have printed money, Argentina and Venezuela style, causing massive hyperinflation.) We are seeing reforms like these in Argentina where President Javier Milei is gutting the government after decades of reckless spending, corruption, and hyperinflation that destroyed Argentina.

A potentially positive development is Elon Musk and Vivek Swamy creating the DOGE (Department of Government Efficiency), where they want to weed out massive waste and cut spending rapidly and gut the bureaucratic elite, similar to what Milei is doing in Argentina. If they can do these things, I think that we might save ourselves from a massive debt crisis. There will be pain before gain. Right now the federal government spends over $7 trillion a year, which is nearly 25% of GDP. If you were to cut $1 trillion–$2 trillion of that, you would be taking about 3.5% to 7% of spending out of the economy; and while over the longer term this would help growth, taking this money out short term would probably cause a recession.

A fear I have is there are still numerous big government Republicans that could vote down massive spending cuts.

What could happen could be similar to what Reagan did in 1980 with interest rates. He allowed Paul Volker to raise interest rates to stop inflation. This did cause a very steep recession from 1981 to 1982, but then a 20-year economy boom afterwards! I would suspect if the Trump administration does massive government cuts, it will cause a similar deep recession and bear market in the short term (U.S. equities, as you will read, are near all-time highs in valuation), which would be much more expensive than in 1981. In the long term such cuts and shrinking the size of government could set the stage for a sustainable long-term boom.

In 2005, right at the top of the U.S. real estate market, Hurricane Katrina ravaged New Orleans. This led to many problems in the insurance industry, which did not cover much of the flooding damage. As the real estate boom occurred in many coastal areas, it led to problems with insurance and played a part in real estate topping in 2005 and crashing into 2009.

In early 2025, wild fires are ravaging Los Angeles and California in one of the biggest natural disasters in American history. These disasters often occur before major economic crises as they can expose flaws in the economy system. The 1906 San Francisco earthquake caused money to move from the U.S. Treasury to California to pay for the rebuilding of San Francisco and led to a liquidity crunch, which helped lead to the 1907 panic and stock market crash of the time.

This natural disaster is occurring in some of the most expensive real estate in the United States and ravaging the insurance industry with 10s if not 100s of billions of dollars in damages that I believe will help lead to a top in the current property market bubble and help lead the economy lower into 2026! Approximately 20% of all home insurance coverage is sold in California, so these fires will have an effect (the home insurance stocks have been tanking the last few days).

This book is not doom and gloom. While the current state of the global economy is indeed alarming, you must not let the failure of large governments and multinational corporations to properly manage their funds negatively affect your investment decisions. In fact, quite the opposite—with the bursting of the bubble, great opportunities will arise for the informed investor. The world financial system is experiencing serious changes in terms of emerging technologies, fluctuating commodities, precious metals markets, and debt-servicing capabilities. Even the fiat system is evolving with the developments and implementation of cryptocurrencies globally. With so many rapidly emerging and changing markets and sectors of the economy, many opportunities will present themselves for financial gain in the short and long term alike.

John Templeton, whom I consider a mentor, famously said, "You want to buy at the point of maximum pessimism." Much of this book is about finding these bargains and profiting from when assets become cheap.

will [illegible] a drop in the current property market and [illegible] may lead the economy lower in 2020. Approximately 25% of all home insurance coverage is sold in California, [illegible] these fires will have an effect (the home insurance [illegible] have been [illegible] the [illegible] new [illegible].

This book is not doom and gloom. While the current state of the global economy [illegible] the [illegible] for the future of the governments and multinational corporations to properly manage [illegible] in their decisions. In fact, quite the opposite — with the bursting of the bubble, great opportunities will arise for the [illegible]. The world has never [illegible] such [illegible] changes. In the [illegible] technologies, [illegible] commodities, precious metals, [illegible] with [illegible] and implementation of [illegible] globally [illegible] rapidly [illegible] changing [illegible] and sectors of the economy, many opportunities will present themselves for [illegible] alike.

John Templeton, who [illegible] considered [illegible] said, "The [illegible] at the point of maximum pessimism." [illegible] this book [illegible] these [illegible] and [illegible].

MEGA RETURNS

1

Investment Grade Corporate Debt—the Next Big Short

Before we get into the nitty-gritty of the investment grade corporate markets, let's first define investment grade corporate bonds, and second, let's look at why we feel investment grade corporate bonds are the next "big short" in terms of mispricing and potential leverage on trading.

Companies that have manageable levels of debt, good earnings potential, and good debt-paying records will have good credit ratings. Investment grade refers to the quality of a company's credit.

Investment grade corporate bond ETFs (exchange-traded funds) offer exposure to high-quality corporate bonds. Investment grade bonds are defined as having a credit rating of BBB or higher, which means they are at a very low risk of default. Half of the $12 trillion corporate bond market is made up of investment grade corporations with about $6 trillion rated as investment grade.

GROWTH OF DEBT

Investment grade corporate debt usually arises from companies that are extremely secure and seemingly safe, that is, Fortune 500 companies. However, when global central banks began to suppress rates using quantified easing (QE), this "shocked" corporate bonds, essentially giving large corporations a very cheap and easy way to borrow money. Figure 1.1 shows the interest rate of investment rollover over the next few years. We can see that from 2025 to 2027, $2.6 trillion of corporate debt will mature, meaning it will probably be rolled over. Much of this debt was issued at near-zero rates in the 2015–2021 period and will be rolled over at much higher rates (even with U.S. Federal Reserve rate cuts that will occur from late 2024 into 2025).

The low interest rates have caused these large companies to become extremely leveraged. Additionally, many of these companies used this leverage on stock buybacks. Here are a few examples of large-cap companies that have taken on an extreme amount of debt, and how this money was spent on buybacks:

- McDonald's saw long-term debt increase from $24 billion to $53 billion between the years 2015 and 2023. This is an increase of over 100% in just eight years! At the same time, McDonald's revenue decreased from $25 billion to $21 billion, a decrease of roughly 16%! This tells you that the company is extremely leveraged.
- Another American Fortune 500 brand, 3M has seen its debt rise from $8.7 billion to over $13 billion. This is an increase of nearly 60% in the same eight-year period. Additionally, 3M's revenues are up only 8% in the same time frame from $30.2 billion to $32.7 billion. Again, like McDonald's, 3M is extremely leveraged.
- One of the "lay-investor's" favorite growth stocks is Boeing, which unsurprisingly, has grown its long- and short-term

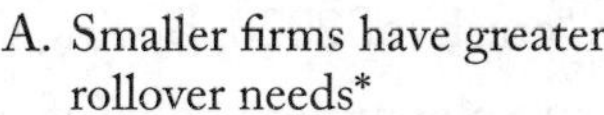

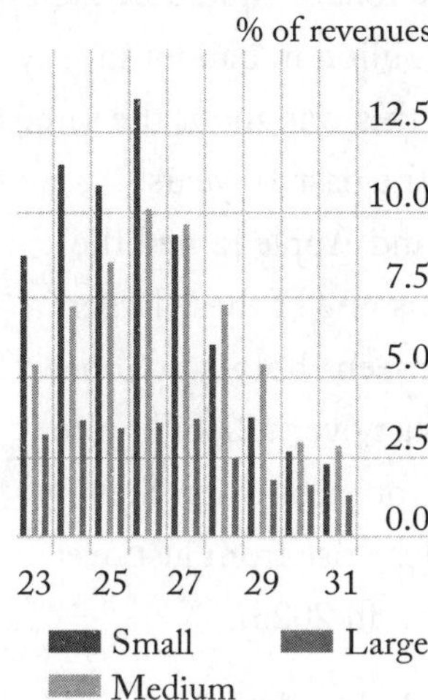

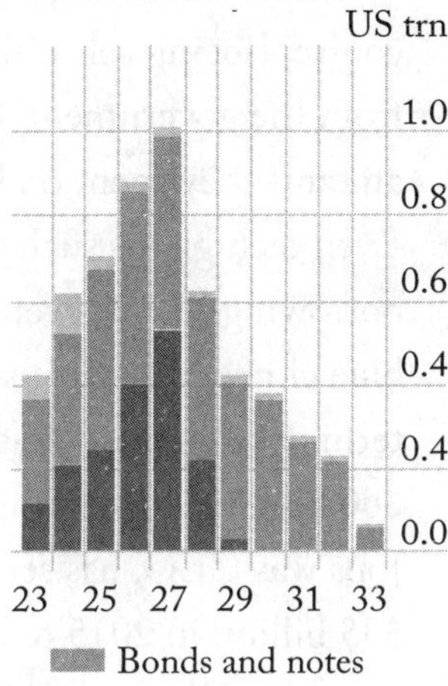

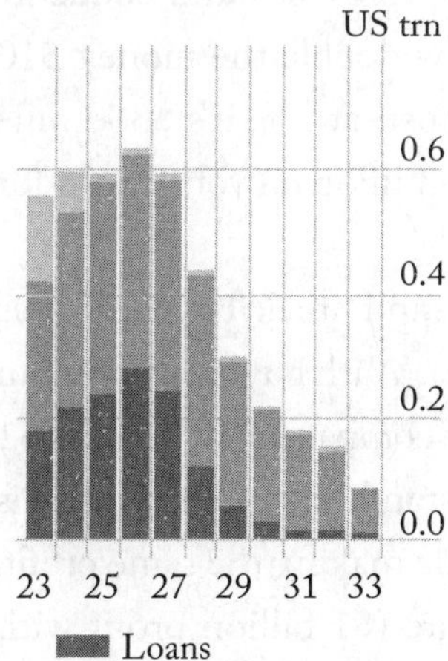

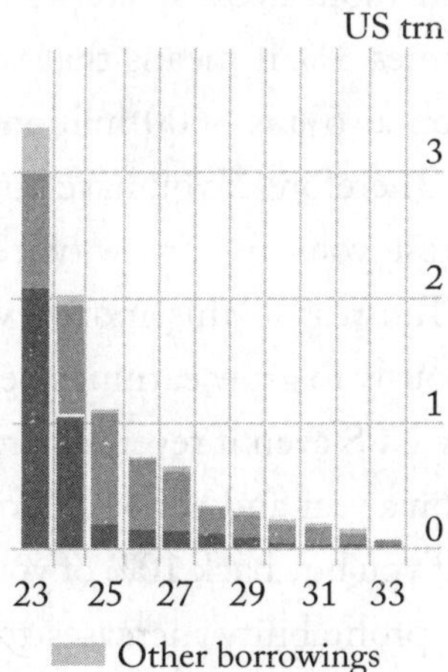

* Small/medium/large = in the bottom/middle/top tercile of 2022 revenues in the respective country.

FIGURE 1.1 Rollover of corporate debt until 2033.
Source: S&P Capital IQ. Courtesy of https://www.bis.org/publ/qtrpdf/r_qt2312w.htm

debt from $7.5 billion to $37 billion from 2015 to 2023, an increase of nearly 400%! During the "crash" of 2020, Boeing's business tanked as global travel came to a complete halt. Of course, Boeing asked for nearly $65 billion in bailout money from the government. Unbelievably, this was about the same amount they spent on buybacks for the past 10 years.

- Even tech giants such as Microsoft and Apple joined the borrowing mania, even more so than some of these larger blue chips. Microsoft since 2015 has seen short- and long-term debt increase drastically, from just over $27 billion to $60 billion! Apple, which didn't take on debt when Steve Jobs was CEO, has seen corporate debt rise from just over $55 billion in 2015 to over $81 billion in 2023.

The reason that companies can afford this debt is very simple: credit is cheap, and with low underlying interest costs, you can afford more debt. If corporate debt is typically 6% and suddenly becomes 3%, it means that you can borrow double the money. $10 billion at 6% is $600 million in interest cost; at 3%, it's $300 million. Therefore, if you have budgeted $600 million on your books for interest, you can borrow twice as much!

The reason this money was used to fund stock buybacks was obviously to grow earnings per share (EPS). With buybacks, you can grow EPS even if revenues are stagnant. If company ABC makes $1 billion a year and has $1 billion shares outstanding, the share price is $1. If you buy back 10% of your shares while making the same profit, your profitability increases to $1.11 a share ($1 billion profit with 900 million shares outstanding), although the company failed to grow the bottom line. It doesn't matter how much cash and option packages are linked to EPS—the growth on the buybacks inevitably fills the pockets of insiders and board members of these companies.

Microsoft had 10.9 billion shares outstanding in 2005. It now has 7.4 billion outstanding, a substantial decrease of roughly 35% in 19 years! If Microsoft were to buy back 3.5 billion shares every 19 years, they wouldn't have any shares left in roughly 50 years. When you look at buybacks from this perspective, you begin to see how ludicrous and unsustainable they are and were in the first place.

Overall, investment grade corporate debt has grown from just over $3 trillion before the financial crisis in 2007 to over $6 trillion today.

MISPRICING OF RISK

This is where the Big Short trade comes in. As we can see from companies such as Apple and Microsoft, many large corporations operated by accruing debt for the last several years—it's no secret. The only reason this debt is sustainable is because interest rates are near an all-time low. These historically low interest rates give these large corporations the ability to take on more debt while retaining the same interest payment. Mismanagement of debt can lead to balance sheet and interest payment problems which can also eat into earnings and margins. They must spend more on servicing this debt rather than investing in research and development, new technologies, or expansion.

Look at mortgage-backed securities (MBS) in 2006. The market had never witnessed a major problem in investment grade corporate debt, and the market pricing and investors failed to anticipate that investment grade debt could see a major decline in price. So when interest rates for AAA-rated securities skyrocketed and they declined in price, it made the MBS worthless. Hundreds of billions were lost, and it nearly bankrupted the entire financial sector.

It should be noted that investment grade debt operates differently than government debt. Historically we have witnessed a so-called flight-to-safety trade in times of economic recession. A flight-to-safety trade means investors will put money into larger, more liquid government bonds on the assumption their bond markets are, well, secure, safe, and liquid. This was evident when in the recession of 2008, U.S. treasuries, U.K. treasuries, German treasuries, Canadian treasuries, and Australian treasuries all increased in price, whereas corporate debt declined in price.

Corporations operate much *differently* than governments in times of economic crisis. In a recession, business takes a hit. Corporations see declines in revenues and profits. This causes investors to do two things: (1) sell corporate bonds, as their businesses are more dependent on the economy, and (2) buy government bonds, which are regarded as safe and liquid.

While governments and treasuries jointly battled the financial crisis, investment grade corporate bonds did not. The implied yield of investment grade corporate bonds with a 7- to 10-year time frame went from 6% to over 10%! This implied yield is currently 4.3%, the all-time low being 3.2%. Before the financial crisis, this yield had never been below 4%—that gives you some historical context on just how low yields were at their recent all time lows. Once again, these unprecedented fluctuations can be attributed to the large-scale mispricing of debt.

This mispricing of debt was discussed by Peter Gundlach, financial analyst and international bond manager, in a presentation in May of 2019. Here are some of the key takeaways.

According to Gundlach, corporate bonds have been "rich by one standard deviation for most of the last three years," and were at an "outright sell" level. A massive amount of corporate debt is weighing on the corporate bond market, and a lot of bonds are "complacently owned." Gundlach cited a Morgan Stanley report that showed that the oversupply and weak ratings standards could lead to downgrades. According to this report and Gundlach's leverage ratios, 38% of the corporate bond market should be rated uninvestable. This quite simply means that if and when rates stabilize from today's uncharacteristically cheap levels, 38% of the investment grade corporate bond market would not be regarded as investment grade. Gundlach feels that "this could mirror what happened to the subprime market during the financial crisis, in terms of the misrating of bonds." He went on to note that the corporate bond market was five times the size of the subprime market prior to the crisis, although not as mispriced. In concurrence with Gundlach, clearly, the mispricing of risk poses a serious threat to the corporate bond market.

The corporate bond market is mispriced due to a false sense of security, founded upon the fact that historically, investment grade corporate bonds have been stable—and investors feel they will continue to be stable. However, operating under the pretense that things will continue to be stable is an extremely dangerous game to play, especially when it involves your money. If and when this relationship breaks, and the investment grade corporate bond bubble is exposed yet again, there will be great opportunities in shorting MBS, much like the Big Short investors did in years prior.

THE LQD INSTRUMENT FOR THE NEXT BIG SHORT

One of the issues for your average investor is that the Big Short–type trades are only readily available for larger, more sophisticated investors. However, the trade that I believe will be the *next* Big Short involves simple investment grade corporate bonds that the average investor can easily execute. Yes, we are talking about shorting investment grade bonds. I think junk bonds, which have also prospered from "cheap money" and the search for yield will fall. I undoubtedly believe that the paramount of mispriced assets are corporate bonds.

As demonstrated earlier, companies have been on a borrowing spree by taking advantage of low rates. Nevertheless, we believe there is a grave mispricing of these risks that will inevitably lead to another great "Big Short trade." Here's why:

- Due to government interest rates having traded at historically low levels in 2020 and 2021, the premium that investors will pay for corporate bonds has diminished. Due to this, corporate bond debt is trading at artificially high levels, especially with the increased debt listed on many corporations' balance sheets. This is a mispricing of risk due to low long-term government interest rates (which is the starting point for interest-bearing products) leading corporate bonds to yield much lower returns than expected.
- In an economic downturn, corporations sell less, and profit margins are squeezed and/or disappear. Moreover, it's harder to meet interest payments or even pay back debt, as corporate bonds roll over in any economic downturn. Combine this with the extraordinarily high debt levels, and companies will find it extremely difficult to service this debt. Furthermore, corporate interest rates typically decline and disconnect from government bond yields as they usually do in economic recession.
- We're facing an issue where corporate debt is going to roll over in the coming years. Most of the corporate bonds that were issued during the cheap money boom of the last 10 years were 5 to 10 years in length. These bonds will have to be repaid or rolled over at some point in the next 6 years till 2030. Many of these companies I mentioned previously that have seen huge increases in debt since 2015 have seen decreases since 2022 because the cost of the borrowing is so

much higher now. If companies must continue to deleverage the next 6 years, it could mean less stock buybacks and financial engineering and lower stock prices.

- The Fed buying "corporate bond ETFs"—a strategy many criticize as ineffective—raises the question, "Why are you shorting the Fed when they are funding investment grade bonds via EFT purchases?" My reasoning is this: many of these bonds will be downgraded in the coming months and years. When bonds are devalued so quickly, it means the investment grade funds are forced to sell in a market with very few buyers. When they do sell, the prices drop, while still in the LQD and other ETFs that desperately need to be unloaded. This will cause them to drop in price, which is my obvious reason for deciding to short them.

CORPORATE BONDS SHORT IDEA

Before the financial crisis, MBS were generally regarded as a safe investment. Virtually everyone paid their mortgage, and when you bundled millions of mortgages together, the chance that enough would be defaulted on to make the entire security worthless was astronomically low. Investment grade corporate bonds have always been viewed as safe because we have yet to witness a major crisis in this market in our lifetime. However, we have never seen these corporations go on a borrowing spree like they have in the last 10 years, and many would say that the crash has been a long time coming, that these debts are set to roll over any day now.

Having identified this potential burst in the corporate bond market, how do we short it? I believe the answer to that lies in buying puts on the LQD corporate bond ETF.

Here's a quick lesson in options before we begin. An option, in a nutshell, is when one purchases a contract to buy or sell a stock, usually 100 shares per contract, at a prenegotiated price by a certain date. The date part is significant here because there are two different types of options: puts and calls. A put is a bet that a stock will fall in price at the agreed-upon date, whereas a call bets that it will rise in price. For the sake of this trade, we are simply going to be buying a put option. If we were to go into writing, selling, or the many complicated possibilities of the options markets, we would need another book in its entirety.

When one is purchasing an option, there is usually a premium involved. This is known as implied volatility. In layman's terms, a stock's volatility refers to its stability. Highly volatile stocks are risky and tend to fluctuate quickly. Some stocks are more volatile than others, and a higher implied volatility means a higher premium on the option of that security when purchasing.

Let me give you a brief relevant example. Netflix is an undeniably volatile stock. As I write in 2024, Netflix is trading at $670 per share; the Netflix January 2025 $600 put options are just $70 out of money and trade at $33, meaning that Netflix must trade at $567 in January 2025 just to break even. This is a perfect example of implied volatility.

The higher the volatility of a stock, the higher the implied volatility. When combined with highly volatile options, this creates a difficult climate in which to turn a substantial profit, as you need large movement in one direction. Obviously, this is extremely hard to predict. For example, if Netflix dropped $100 to $570 at the date of expiration, those $60 puts would trade at roughly $30—which puts your investment only barely at roughly the level they trade at now! This seems like a high-risk, low-reward situation—but the key in turning profits on derivatives is to *seek out mispricing*.

The Big Short traders took advantage of mispricing when they noticed that the credit defaults swaps on MBS, rated AA and AAA, had been priced based on zero chance of default. Yet when you looked beneath the surface and considered restarts of teaser rates and back-ended mortgages, the leveraging of these instruments showed there was a real risk that these bonds would begin to fail in 2006 and 2007.

While implied volatility has picked up with "corporate bond ETF'S" during the crash of 2020 (as they historically are safe), the Fed now claims they will buy because the implied volatility of ETFs is lower than many stocks and other sectors of the market.

Presently, the LQD trades at $106 in 2024, the January 2025 $100 puts are only $6 and just over 5% out of the money-only trade at $0.65 per option. The implied volatility is just 9.7% (there is not a large amount of implied volatility in LQD options). If you happened to get a big move in corporate bonds to, say, $90 (15% bust), while there was a concurrent recession or a blowout in corporate rates as the market readjusts, that would be a 16x profit with the puts going roughly $10 in the money at $90.

Historically, when there are fluctuations and crashes in the market, investors panic and premiums blow out. When the Big Short sellers sold many of the credit default swaps, not only did they sell at a huge premium, but they were selling to people who were overpaying for insurance, panicking as MBS failed. Consequently, I would expect if there were to be a big move in corporate bonds, not only would they go in the money, but the implied volatility and premiums would blow out as investors panic. Let's say for argument's sake that the premium on these puts jumps from 10% to 20%. That would mean the premium of the 100s would be roughly $10. Combine that with the $10 in the money, and you get roughly $20. In sum, if there was just a 15% drop in the corporate bond market, you'd make your money back 30 times over.

This isn't just playing short-term options, or options that are way out of the money; you are buying options that expire roughly nine months in the future and are only 5% of the money. (As this book is going to press in December 2024, if the corporate bond market has not rolled over by then, I would recommend January 2026 puts, as that will give you a 13-month time frame for a sell-off in investment grade corporate bonds.)

With this trade, let me remind you we are betting that investment grade corporate debt will be one of the epicenters of the current upcoming recession. In the last recession, the epicenter was mortgage debt and MBS. Now that the leverage has been built up on balance sheets involving substantial investment grade corporate debt, this bubble is predestined to burst in the same manner as the mortgage crisis.

Our reasoning for this trade is that these investment grade corporate bonds are greatly mispriced, and when the recession hits, the debt will be exposed. If they are downgraded to junk and the LQD and other funds must sell the bonds that are not investment grade, all the Fed buying in the world won't help them. There is an old saying: "When the tide goes, you see who is naked."

A great thing about this trade is that you, the average investor, can do it. Unlike the complex CDS trades of the 2000s, all you will need is a margin account to buy the puts for this trade.

Of course, I must warn you that you do not need to try to be a hero with this trade. With over $5 trillion in corporate debt being rolled over from 2024 to 2030, you do not know what year a potential bust will come. The Fed is buying bonds, which could delay the big drawdown in investment grade corporates. Could it be in 2025, 2026, 2027? Who knows? View this trade like buying insurance on your car or house. Do it as a sort of "ultimate" insurance. Every year keep buying a few long-dated put options on the LQD. When the day of reckoning comes, the profit from these options should hedge your portfolio in a downturn and maybe even make you a bit of money. I am not trying to make you rich; I am trying to keep you wealthy.

2

The Everything Bubble

In the past few decades, the economy has experienced numerous bubbles and busts. In the early 2000s we saw the explosion of the dot-com bubble, and more recently in 2007 the burst of the housing market bubble. Today, we are experiencing the "everything bubble." Nearly every asset class is at a historical all-time high—stocks, bonds, and real estate alike. This can mainly be attributed to the cheap money policies of the Fed and inflation due to a massive increase in money printing. This everything bubble creates a new series of issues regarding traditional investments; however, as we will discuss throughout the rest of this chapter, I believe there will be a variety of opportunities for the savvy investor.

We must ask ourselves, why did everything in the United States collapse so quickly following the Covid crisis? A pandemic like Covid should not cause the global economy and markets to be so volatile. In 1918 to 1919, the Spanish flu killed nearly 2% of the entire world's population; 600,000 in the United States alone. In 1957 we had the Asian flu, closely followed by the Hong Kong flu in 1968. Currently, we haven't yet seen the end of the Covid flu; therefore we can't speculate as to how many people it will kill. All things considered, it's fair to say Covid wasn't nearly as deadly as the other pandemics, but its effect on the economy is unlike anything we've ever seen to date.

The pandemic phase of Covid is now over, but there are a few things we know: the economy was not as strong as advertised; it was built upon a mirage of cheap money and debt. Businesses, governments, and even individuals were taking advantage of the leverage and stock markets. The issue is that the stock market was extremely overvalued! Vulnerable to any sort of economic slowdown, let alone a "supervirus" that shuts down global commerce. It is just as overvalued now, so again it will be susceptible to any potential slowdown.

In past booms, you had one or two sectors of the market that really contributed to the bubble. In the 1920s, it was the equity crisis; in the 1970s, it was a commodity crisis; in the 1980s, junk bonds and corporate real estate were issues; in the 1990s, it was emerging market equities, then tech stocks, followed up with the residential real estate mortgage crisis in the 2000s.

The most recent bubble of the last 15 years was created not by economic strength but rather by monetary money printing. The main goal of quantitative easing (QE) was to inflate asset prices and re-create a "wealth effect," which serves to benefit the rich (as they own most assets). This was guided mainly by the principles of trickle-down economics, hoping that upper-class spending and investments would help stimulate the economy across all social classes.

From 2008 to 2019, the Federal Reserve's balance sheet increased from just over $600 billion to over $3 trillion, the European Central Bank's balance sheet grew from $1.5 trillion to over $3 trillion, and the Japanese Central Bank's balance sheet grew from over 100 trillion yen to over 500 trillion! Since Covid, the Fed's balance sheet soared from that $3 trillion to over $6 trillion and sits at $5.7 trillion as of July 2024.

The most obvious recipient of cheap money was the stock market. As discussed in Chapter 1, much of the printed money depressed interest rates, which filtered down to the investment grade corporate bond market. Subsequently, these corporations took advantage by borrowing at cheap rates and using that money to buy back stock, which inflated the stock's price.

Additionally, if you have depressed fixed-income rates, it causes people to pay a premium for growth. One reason the so-called Magnificent Seven stocks trade at such large premiums is simply because investors are willing to pay these premiums. In a world devoid of real growth or real interest rates, people are willing to pay top dollar to get into growing markets. Despite making very little in terms of the bottom line, investors will pay whatever for the top-line growth experienced by companies such as Amazon and Netflix in recent years.

LONG-TERM INDICATORS: THE BUFFETT INDICATOR, PRICE TO SALES, AND THE CAPE RATIO

Two of my favorite indicators for stock valuations are the stock market cap as a percentage of GDP (known as the Buffett Indicator) and price to sales.

As mentioned earlier, the problem with looking at price-to-earnings ratios as a metric of valuation is that financial engineering and buyback of stock (happening in real time) are inflating earnings per share (EPS) numbers. As the number of shares continues to decline, the market looks cheaper than it is.

However, two things cannot be fabricated: market cap and gross sales.

Market Cap to GDP

Market cap to GDP historically trades around 75%, meaning the stock market is roughly three-quarters of the size of the entire economy. (See Figure 2.1.) At the market's peak in February 2020, it traded at 155% of GDP, an all-time high! Only two times prior has the stock market cap traded over 100% of GDP (indicating that the market is larger than the economy). These numbers have only been seen in 2000 during the height of the tech bubble and 2007 right before the global financial crisis. In each case, S&P 500 stocks dropped over 50% from their highs. In 2021 it went to 200% of GDP, an all-time high, and the S&P dropped 25% in 2022. In the fall of 2024, it traded to over 205% , which has surpassed the 2021 all-time high (the S&P 500 dropped nearly 30%, reaching that level in late 2021). This tells us that from this ratio stocks could be in for a hefty decline.

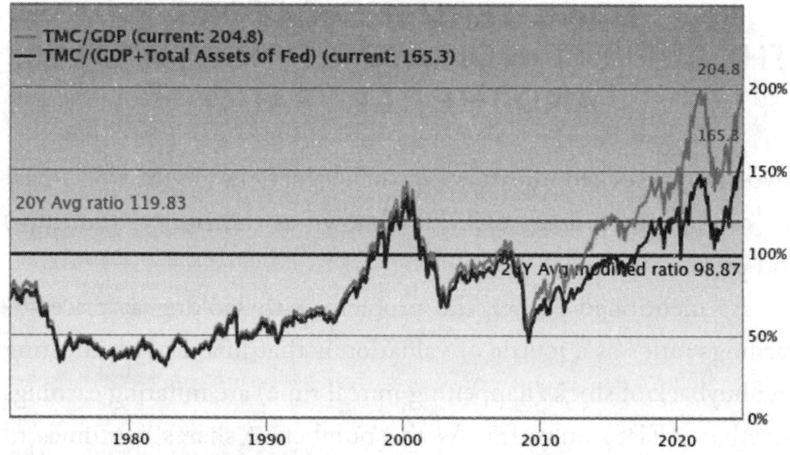

FIGURE 2.1 Market cap to GDP.
Source: www.gurufocus.com

Price to Sales

The price-to-sales ratio is like price to earnings; however, instead of calculating the price of the stock compared to earnings, you compare it to sales. I prefer the price-to-sales ratio because you cannot manipulate the top line like you can the bottom line through accounting gimmicks or financial engineering. It's either your stock prices are growing faster than your sales or they're not.

Historically, the market has traded around 1.3 times sales. (See Figure 2.2.) One time the market traded over 3.0 times sales; that was the 2021 post-Covid bubble. In the fall of 2024, it is again trading over 3.0 times sales right now the all-time highs of late 2021, which also tells us the market could be in for a hefty decline.

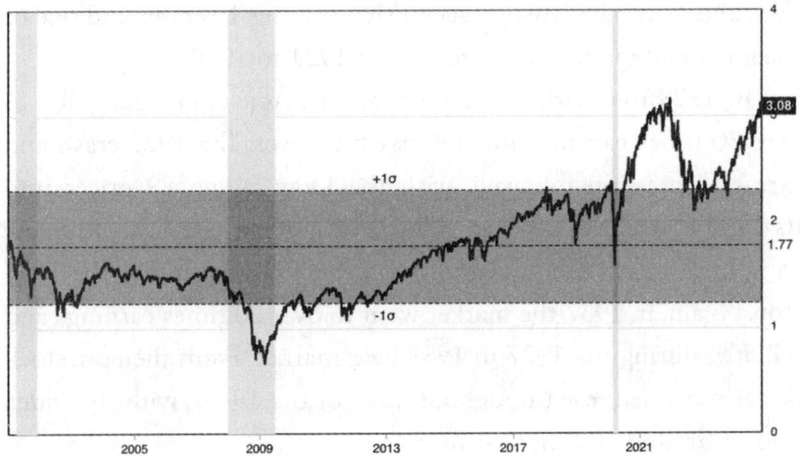

FIGURE 2.2 S&P 500 price-to-sales ratio.
Source: www.gurufocus.com

Case-Shiller PE

The final indicator we will look at is the Case-Shiller PE. Figure 2.3 shows the Case-Shiller PE ratio. This is a ratio that smooths out valuations. Rather than just looking at PEs over the last quarter or year, it looks at the 10-year average of the PE. This is a way to smooth out valuation and an excellent way to predict longer-term returns.

Historically, the market trades around 16 times earnings. Anything over 20 and especially over 25 on the Case-Shiller PE ratio demonstrates the market is overvalued. Anything under 15 (especially 13) is cheap. If you get the 10-year moving average under 10, then it is extremely cheap.

The first period of elevated valuations dates to the early 1900s when the ratio got around 25 times earnings. This preceded the panic of 1907, with stocks entering a near-14-year bear market falling to 1921. In 1921 the index was at its cheapest, going down to five times earnings! This preceded the Roaring Twenties and one of the great bull markets in history from 1921 to 1929.

In 1929 the market's 10-year ratio became stretched, going to over 30 times earnings for the first time ever. The 1929 crash and Great Depression followed, with the Dow falling 89 prices into its 1932 bottom. This huge decline made stocks cheap, as the Dow went up nearly 5 times in price from the 1932 bottom to the 1937 stop. Again, in 1937 the market went to over 20 times earnings and fell 50% during the 1937 to 1939 bear market. From then on, stock prices remained low throughout most of the 1940s, with the index trading around 10 times earnings.

This led to the 1949–1966 post-war "boom" when stock prices soared. Then from 1966 to 1982 the market went to over 25 times earnings. Stocks lost nearly 75% of their value and became cheap again (when adjusted for inflation). In 1982 the Case-Shiller index fell to 6 times earnings, its third cheapest reading ever. However, this preceded the huge bull market of 1982 to 2000, with the Dow climbing nearly 1,400 percent!

In 2000 the index traded out of control. Many stocks in the S&P were tech and dot-com stocks with little to no earnings. The influence of these stocks on the S&P caused the P/E to soar! The Case-Shiller PE traded to a (current) record of 45 times earnings in 2000!

With all this being said, this indicator is not perfect. If you had followed it, you would have sold in the late 1990s and missed the last blow-off in the markets. However, it should be noted that from 1997 to the market's low in 2009, the market fell after the Case-Shiller PE reached an extreme valuation. If you had been patient and sold the market in the late 1990s when it was overvalued, then bought back in 2009 when it got undervalued, you would have been buying the market much lower (especially when adjusted for inflation).

In 2009 the Case Schiller PE index hit 15, marking the lowest reading since the late 1980s! Of course, this brings us to the unprecedented bull market that has made up the last 10 years.

Again, the ratio is demonstrating extreme valuations, trading at near-40 times earnings as I write in the fall of 2024. There are only three other times in history the valuation has been this high . . . with 1929, 2000, and 2021 being the other three. This ratio is warning us about a potential significant decline in the markets, like 1929, 2000, and 2021 in which bear markets followed.

All three of these indicators demonstrate that the market would have to drop a further 40% to 50% to get back to historical norm valuations. This is also a conservative estimate, as the market usually overshoots to the downside. For example, in 2009 price to sales, stocks hit 0.8 (about 40% below the historical median).

In the early 1980s, just before stocks began their bull market, market cap to GDP was about 40%, about 35% below the historical median. The Case-Shiller PE went to the single digits in 1921, 1932, the 1940s, and early 1980s, roughly half of its historical median. (See Figure 2.3.) This current massive overvaluation should be followed by a bear market and period where stocks trade at a discount to historical lows.

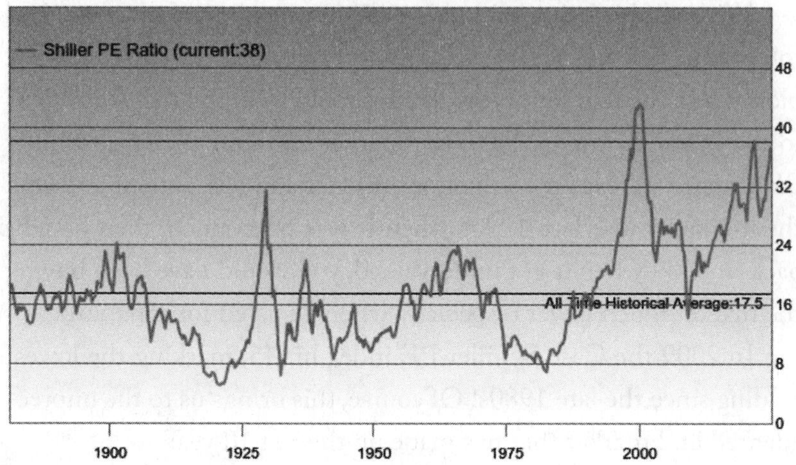

FIGURE 2.3 S&P 500 Case-Shiller PE ratio.
Source: www.gurufocus.com

PASSIVE INVESTING BUBBLE

An offshoot of the equity bubble is the passive investing bubble. The economy had been in a bull market cycle for a 10-year period; nearly a decade of gains with little volatility left investors feeling as though they could play the market risk-free. With the resolution of the 2009 economic crisis, we witnessed two large corrections of 15% to 20% in the markets in 2010 and 2011, respectively. Then in late 2012, the Fed went full in with QE printing, generating well over $1 trillion new bills between 2012 and 2014. There was a small drawdown of about 13% in 2015 to early 2016, then one final correction in 2018. Before the crash of March 2020 due to the unprecedented Covid pandemic, the bull market had lasted 11 years, making it the longest on record. Typically, there is a 10% correction every year and a bear market every 3 to 5 years, so this extended bull period helps justify why investors felt so little risk at the time.

Kyle Bass is an important name to know: he is currently the founder and principal of Hayman Capital, a Dallas-based hedge fund focused on global events. However, you may recognize him as the famed fund manager who made a fortune during the 2008 financial crisis. Bass purchased credit default swaps on subprime securities in anticipation of the mortgage crisis, and when the real estate bubble burst, he made a killing in profits. Bass believes that the typical investor's perspective when investing mostly revolves around their last two years, meaning the average investor tends to anticipate a market and trends that were observable over their past two years of investing, rather than broadening their scope of reference. Not only do I agree with this theory, but I think this line of thinking was the driving force behind the passive investing bubble.

This was seen in fund flows. An exchange-traded fund (ETF) is an investment fund traded on stock exchanges, much like stocks. ETFs can hold bonds, stocks, commodities, and volatility options on whatever industry they are reflecting the performance of. However, the difference between an ETF and a mutual fund is that the ETF fund manager does not pick or choose the stocks individually. Rather an ETF operates based on the index it represents (i.e., if it's the S&P 500 or Russell 2000), or an ETF may allocate stocks to the asset class it represents (i.e., owns gold stocks if it is a gold stock ETF, oil stocks if it's an oil ETF, tech or stocks if it's a tech ETF). An ETF is essentially a portfolio of assets in a specific sector. Mutual funds are essentially hedge funds that charge much higher fees than ETFs. A mutual fund manager is trying to outperform the markets with stock selection or outperform in downturns by raising cash when markets become overvalued.

Hedge funds use long- and short-term strategies to profit from the increase or decrease in stock price. However, this strategy depends on two main factors to be profitable: volatility in the markets and the ability to short stocks. When the market is continually climbing with no major corrections for extended periods of time, it's very difficult to short stocks. This meant that in the last decade-long bull period, hedge funds had a more difficult time predicting the market. By the nature in which they operate, hedge funds and mutual funds must be actively managed and require much more attention; therefore, they charge higher fees to their clients. These fees and the psychology mentioned earlier by Bass led some investors to lean toward ETFs rather than hedge or mutual funds. Interestingly, in 2020 as the Covid pandemic rocked the economy, hedge funds and mutual funds alike vastly outperformed ETFs—mainly due to the decrease in price observed by some volatile major corporations. That was the first major decline in some time for some of these corporations.

Owning and investing mainly in ETFs is not much different than indexing, where you are just basically pinning your investment performance to the major U.S. indexes (Dow Jones Industrial Average, S&P 500, and NASDAQ). It is currently estimated that nearly 45% of the market is passive investment–owned, with another 25% of the bond market being passive investment–owned as well.

The main reason why the current trend in passive investment is so problematic involves if and when there is another recession. Ultimately, it's only a matter of time. Most of these ETFs' portfolios are nearly identical and many times contain the same stocks. Thus, when a recession occurs and ETFs try to unload their portfolios, they flood the market with an influx of the same stocks, causing prices to plummet and damaging ETFs across the board. In addition, by their nature, ETFs tend to have virtually zero liquidity. Mutual funds can purchase stocks as the market falls, hedge funds have short positions and are able to cover shorts when the market falls, and ETFs are left trying to sell at whatever price they can to cover their losses.

All of this puts into perspective how the stock market bubble has led to the passive investment bubble. It has been so easy to make money in the major indexes in the last decade, and this has changed how a large percentage of the market operates. Being that nearly 45% of the market now operates on ETFs, if a major recession caused these funds to try and sell in mass, it could have serious implications and potentially lead to a downward spiral. As profitable and consistent these ETFs may seem as of recent years' trends, one should strongly urge the investor to keep Kyle Bass's philosophy in mind and not let those years of growth blind them. Don't get me wrong: it is not necessary to steer clear of ETFs altogether, but do continue to diversify your investments across different types of funds to mitigate the effects of the inevitable burst of the passive investment bubble.

NVIDIA: THE POSTER CHILD FOR THE BUBBLE—THE DREADED PARABOLIC CURVE

All bubbles have their poster child for boom and bust. In the 1920s, it was stocks like RCA (radio was a new technology of the day). In the 1970s, there were the Nifty 50 stocks such as IBM and Kodak. In the 1990s, tech, energy, and telecom stocks such as Microsoft, Amazon, Yahoo, Enron, Nortel, WorldCom, and Lucent were the leaders.

In the past few years, we have seen a bubble in the "Fang," which are now named the Magnificent Seven, which feature Apple, Amazon, Nvidia, Alphabet, Meta, Tesla, and Microsoft. These seven stocks now make up nearly 30% of the S&P 500 index as I write in the summer of July, which is a record for any seven stocks to be this large a percentage of the S&P 500.

For the sake of this book, we are just going to concentrate on Nvidia, which I believe is the poster child of this bubble for both its stock chart and the sector it is in (artificial intelligence).

I won't get too much into historical parabolic curves, as I discussed this at length in my book *The Great Super Cycle* and in my fun fiction novel *The Contrarian Who Saved the World*. Basically, a parabolic curve is a stock that starts going up on a near-90° angle near the end of a bear market during a period of mass euphoria. All these curves end the same way with massive crashes. Figure 2.4 shows how the parabolic curve for RCA (the Nvidia of its time in 1929) collapsed during the crash of 1929 and then the depression of the 1930s.

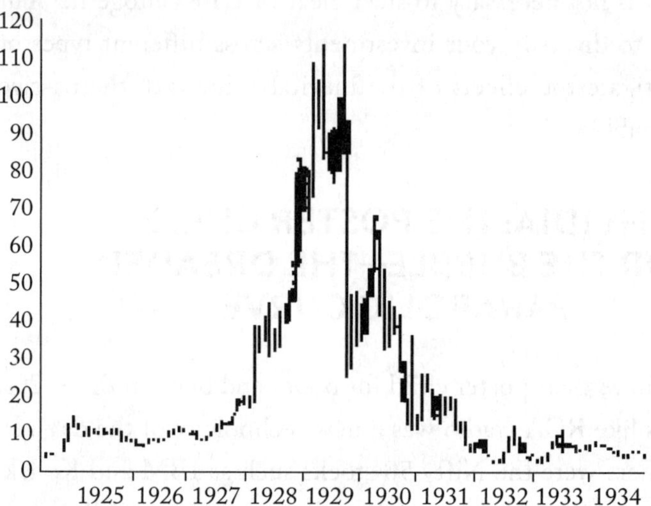

FIGURE 2.4 RCA stock price 1924 to 1934.
Source: https://www.reddit.com/r/BeatTheBear/comments/oxdab1/the_rca_pump_and_dump/

Nvidia has seen a massive increase in price in 2023 and 2024, as its chips are the leading chips for artificial intelligence, or AI as it is known. Artificial intelligence is to our time as the dot-coms were to the 1990s. The fast-growing new technology that will change our lives forever. According to Wikipedia, "AI in its broadest sense is intelligence exhibited by machines, particularly computer systems. It is a field of research in computer science that develops and studies methods and software that enable machines to perceive their environment and use learning and intelligence to take actions that maximize their chances of achieving defined goals."

Nvidia has seen a huge move in its stock price as demand for its chips has skyrocketed. From its low of the 2022 bear market of about $10 a share, Nvidia has soared to near $130 a share! (See Figure 2.5.)

Recently, the Nvidia CEO was featured on *60 Minutes* and is being treated like a rock star, even spotted signing a woman's bra at a tech conference in Asia! This type of mania does not happen at the beginning of bull markets, but rather near the end of euphoric manias. Like RCA in 1929 or Microsoft, Amazon, Lucent, and Oracle in 2000, this parabolic curve will eventually end.

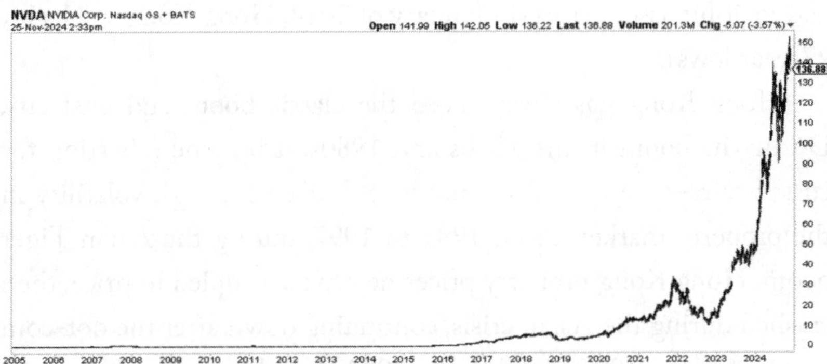

FIGURE 2.5 Nvidia, a classic parabolic curve.
Source: www.stockcharts.com

In the days leading up to this book going up to print, a very important news event happened in regards to NVDA. DeepSeek, a Chinese company, announced basic microchips that are a fraction of the cost. Deepseek announced it had developed AI technology that is comparable, and sometimes even faster, than NVDA's. This caused NVDA stock to drop over 16% on January 27, 2025. Could this be the straw that breaks NVDA's bubble and parabolic curve? Only time will tell.

GLOBAL REAL ESTATE BUBBLES

Another part of the "everything bubble" is, of course, real estate. Especially in certain countries. Take Hong Kong, for example, the epicenter of this bubble; it's in a unique situation of being a world-class global city, a gateway to China, but still heavily reliant on the U.S. monetary system. The Hong Kong dollar is pegged to the U.S. dollar, so they cut rates when the United States does and raise rates when the United States does. So when the United States had cheap money, it helped cause a huge real estate and asset bubble in Hong Kong, whereas when the United States raised rates and Hong Kong had to, it hit asset prices (in January of 2024, Hong Kong stocks hit 27-year lows).

Hong Kong has always been the classic boom-and-bust city. During its boom in the 1970s and 1980s, it became a bastion for laissez-faire–type capitalism and would often see high volatility in the property market. From 1985 to 1997, during the Asian Tiger boom, Hong Kong property prices nearly quadrupled in price, then crashed during the Asian crisis, continuing down after the dot-com bust. From the 1997 highs to the 2003 lows, Hong Kong property fell by over 50%.

As the 2008 financial crisis was mainly concentrated in the West and Hong Kong became more hinged to China, Hong Kong's economy was relatively untouched by this downturn. However, Hong Kong was able to cut rates to near zero, as their monetary system is linked to the United States. From the 2003 lows to the highs in 2018, Hong Kong's real estate prices have more than tripled! From 2003 to 2018, Hong Kong possessed the best of both worlds; they got the boom from China and took advantage of loose U.S. monetary conditions.

Two other countries that benefited from the boom and the loose Chinese monetary policy were Canada and Australia. Historically, the Canadian and Australian banking sectors have been some of the most stable in the world. They have high capital provisions and did not do subprime lending that their U.S. counterparts did during the financial crisis.

Additionally, both are much smaller countries, with Australia's population of 27 million and Canada's 40 million. Much of the demand in their housing markets comes from an influx of wealthy Asians, especially wealthy Chinese. Like Hong Kong, both Australia and Canada have benefited from getting money from the boom in China, but both tend to move interest rates in accordance with the United States, making their interest rates near zero.

Australia is distinguished as having the longest economic expansion in the Western world and not having a recession in nearly 29 years (which ended in 2020)! From the mid-1980s to 2018, Australian prices climbed nearly sevenfold and prices in Sydney, the country's largest city, climbed nearly tenfold!

However, Australia now has a three-pronged problem: (1) slowing of the Chinese economy is causing less money coming into the country, (2) commodity prices are falling, which shows it is a heavily dependent commodity-producing economy, and (3) the country's banks lent aggressively during the housing boom. Nearly 50% of mortgage loans in Australia are interest-only loans. Currently, the banks are converting some of the loans to include principal, as the days of living off housing gains are gone. This is going to put pressure on Australian consumers who are already some of the most indebted in the world.

Canada is in the same boat. Canada's economy has become increasingly less competitive in the last 10 years. Their incoherent policy on pipelines (in Alberta, they want them; in British Columbia, they don't), high taxes, and increasing red tape has led to dissipating foreign investment.

The one thing that Canada got right is they did have a booming property market! Most immigration to Canada was based on economic immigration and large influxes of Chinese, Indian, and Middle Eastern money. Canada's crime rates are lower than its neighbors to the south, and this has attracted plenty of funds for real estate.

Canada is notoriously easy on white-collar crime; thus, as the economy has become increasingly dependent on foreign money in their real estate markets, money laundering is uncontrollable. Vancouver is notorious for having a slew of Chinese money that is just looking to escape China at any price—this isn't investment money; this is money that people want to get out of China as soon as possible.

At the top of the Canadian real estate market, the average price of a home in Vancouver was $2 million. In Toronto, prices are not far behind, with average prices now nearing $1.6 million. Low interest rates have made these housing prices in reach for the average Canadian; many loans in Canada are given out in the form of a line of credit, not a straight-up mortgage. Like the interest-only loans in Australia, there are very few, if zero, principal payments on these loans.

This leverage has built up to the point where Canadians are some of the most indebted people on the planet. Private debt to GDP in Canada is 170% of GDP (it reached roughly only 120% during the peak of the U.S. real estate bubble in 2007).

I have even seen this bubble play out firsthand from my family's own experience. I am from a small town called Dundas, which is about 1 hour south of Toronto, a suburb of Hamilton. It's a picturesque town in a valley surrounded by the Niagara Escarpment. A far cry from the concrete jungle of Toronto, as the town possesses conservation areas, waterfalls, public parks, and the like. Now my town has become a draw for retirement money and high-end retirees. In 2012 my father bought out his siblings and bought his parents' house after they passed away. From 2012 to 2024, the property went up more than sixfold in price! Then my mother purchased a small one-bedroom condo in a higher-end development that tripled in price from 2015 to 2024!

I've noticed all sorts of toys I had never seen before! Middle-aged men driving fancy old-school convertibles (saw a few Stingrays and some Mustangs from the 1960s) and four-wheel bikes. I even saw a DeLorean made up to look like the one in *Back to the Future*! Even with the decline in the Canadian dollar to 70 cents from par with the U.S. dollar, the flights to the Bahamas are full of Canadians. I am sure this is a product of the housing gains and the wealth effect from housing going up a great deal.

Finally, U.S. real estate, while not quite as expensive as Australian and Canadian, has still seen a huge move due to years of near-zero rates. Pre–financial crisis, median U.S. home prices were $258,000 and fell to $208,000 during the financial crisis. They then rebounded to these highs in the mid-2010s and went to about $300,000. Then things really took off post-Covid when zero rates drove everything, going to $440,000; since then, there has been a small decline to $423,000, or roughly a 4% decline. However, when you factor in the rise in rates, going from 3% on a 30-year mortgage to 7%, housing is now about as unaffordable as it has ever been. Figure 2.6 shows the unaffordability of U.S. housing, which is the most unaffordable since the early 1980s when mortgage rates were double digits.

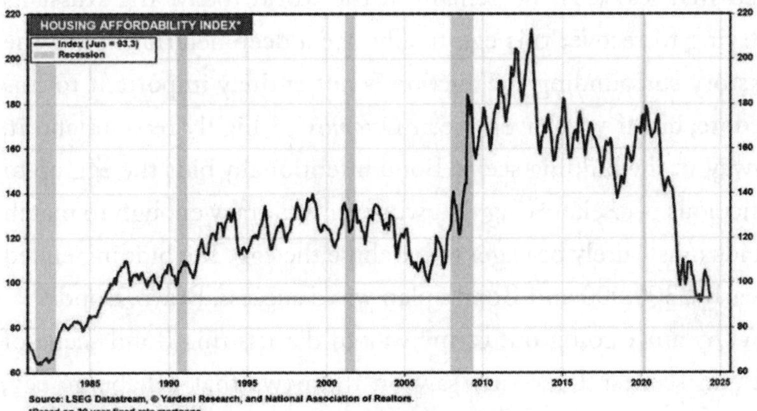

FIGURE 2.6 Unaffordability of housing in the United States.
Source: Yardeni Research. Courtesy of https://x.com/MikeZaccardi/status/1828761139888476463

THE FABERGÉ EGG: FROM JAMES BOND TO A GREAT EXAMPLE OF THE EVERYTHING BUBBLE

Traditional markets are not the only assets that have been inflated by this everything bubble. While stocks and bonds have inflated in price, other forms of investments such as fine art and collectibles have also been affected. A quick anecdote that I think illustrates this comes from the James Bond film series. I am a big Bond fan. Especially the classic Bond movies with Sean Connery and Roger Moore. Pierce Brosnan also played a great Bond, but for this quick illustration, we are going to look at Moore's performance in the 1983 classic *Octopussy*.

Octopussy is my favorite film from the James Bond series, and incidentally it holds a scene that helps illustrate the everything bubble. Bond is on one of his brazen deep cover MI6 spy missions, and he finds himself looking dapper and ritzy at an upscale Sotheby's auction. He is there solely to bid on a Fabergé egg. A Fabergé egg is a collectible antique that was only produced in Russia under the House of Fabergé. There were only about 70 made, and it is estimated that less than 60 remain in the world today. The Russians are trying to recover this egg to advance a deep nefarious plot. The backstory surrounding the auction is not entirely important to this anecdote, but if you haven't seen *Octopussy*, I highly recommend it. Anyway, in the bidding scene, Bond intentionally bids the egg up to a ridiculous price, knowing that whoever was crazy enough to match his bids must surely be eager to purchase the egg. The bidding ended at nearly $300,000 and Bond's plan was a success. Bravo, Bond!

Why am I going out of my way to discuss this Bond scene of all Bond scenes? I recently saw on the news that a Fabergé egg, purchased years ago at a U.S. flea market for $14,000, was now estimated to be worth a staggering $25 million to $33 million! Despite being filmed in 1983, this is still close to 80 to 100 times what the egg from *Octopussy* was evaluated at. Keep in mind, this is a major motion picture and that evaluation itself was most likely exaggerated to make good cinema. My point being, collectibles and fine art are at an all-time high, pricewise. The Dow is up roughly 35 times in the same period. The prices of real estate, jewelry, even fine wine have all soared in the last 35 years. All of this makes the rich richer and causes further inflation of such assets.

What I'm illustrating here is that we really are experiencing an everything bubble—not just a bubble of traditional investments, but a bubble-spanning asset in essentially every category.

Bond ends up completing his MI6 mission and exposing the Russians' villainous plot—but not without getting chastised by his boss for his outlandish bidding. Q chastises him on the premise that had he won the auction, the British government would have had to foot the bill. In hindsight, I think the British government would have been quite happy with getting 100 times return on their fictional investment 41 years later!

HOW TO PROFIT FROM THE BURSTING OF THE EVERYTHING BUBBLE

"OK, David," you might say, "This is fine and dandy, everything from stock prices in the United States, to real estate in Hong Kong, to Canada and Australia. How can I make money off a potential downturn or bust in these bubble assets?" Well, of course, I have some specific ways to do so, including one stock that I think is a perfect play on the bursting of the everything bubble.

For the average investor, the easiest way to hedge your portfolio (outside of my ultimate hedge of the LQD put option short discussed in Chapter 1) is through purchasing bear market funds.

These are funds that trade opposite to the market; that is, they go down in price while the market goes up.

Two actively managed bear funds in the United States are the Bearx and HDGE; Bearx is an actively managed fund that is a mutual fund, and HDGE is an actively managed ETF. Both funds short stocks to take advantage of a decline in stock price.

Of course, there are basic bear ETFs. These are ETFs that just go the opposite of the market; SH is the 1x short of the S&P 500. For more leverage, the SDS is the 2x short of the S&P 500. The RWM is the short fund of the Russell 2000.

The way these funds work is simple: if the S&P or Russell 2000 goes down 1%, the RWM or SH will go up a percent and vice versa. If the S&P goes down 1%, the SDS will go up 2%. This is a very simple way for the average investor to hedge a portfolio if you choose not to do options and the like. As a warning, as the value of these ETFs are reset every day, the leveraged ETFs tend to erode in value, especially if the market continues to trade higher.

Whatever country you're reading this from will have ETFs that trade inversely to domestic markets. In Canada you can buy a TSX/S and P 60 bear, in the United Kingdom a FTSE bear. Therefore, you can hedge against almost any market. These bear funds are the best way for the average investor to protect their portfolio in case the everything bubble bursts and equity prices fall.

There are even ETFs to short individual stocks now. If you think that the bubble in stocks such as NVDA, AMZN, and TSLA will burst, you can purchase ETFs such as NVDS, AMZD, or TSLQ!

In the case of real estate shorts, you could short major banks in Australia, Hong Kong, and Canada. The one issue with this is that these banks have been around forever and have withstood the test of previous booms and busts.

Remember, if there is a problem, the large banks get the bailout first and have more flexibility in changing the rules. For example, in Australia they are starting to charge both interest and principal on mortgages after years of interest-only loans (most of the mortgage agreements contain a clause expressly allowing the lender to do this).

As we are limited in time and space for this book, I am just going to focus on the smaller companies in Canada, which could signal warning signs in the Canadian market (potential shorts) and smaller mortgage lenders that could fail if there is a large enough downturn in the Canadian mortgage market. As I've mentioned, I'm from Canada, so I am comfortable with the market and very familiar with these companies and the risks they have taken in the Canadian economy.

If you are interested in similar smaller-sized shorts in Australia or Hong Kong, you can always subscribe to my newsletter *Maximum Pessimism Investing* (maxpessinvest.com) or the *Financial Intelligence Report*, where I write articles on these subjects from time to time.

The China Effect

Adding to the domino effect is the dwindling of foreign buyers. In Vancouver, the government introduced a 15% tax on foreign purchases. Subsequently, the average home price in Vancouver quickly fell from $1.8 to $1.4 million. They recently announced a similar tax in Toronto, and we have already seen prices decline by over 15% there as well before recovering. In addition, a lot of West Coast real estate in the United States, especially Seattle and San Francisco, have a lot of Chinese money coming into them.

When we look at the current situation in Canada, I think it is important to also look at China very closely. When Japan's market burst in 1990, the Japanese had to go from a net buyer's market to sellers of North American real estate to raise funds. This crushed real estate in cities such as Toronto and New York. If the Chinese need to raise funds as their own economy falters after the effects of Covid, they could become net sellers in Vancouver, Toronto, San Francisco, and Seattle and have the exact same effect on market prices as in the 1990s.

I do not feel the major Canadian banks can escape this looming credit crisis unscathed. This Canadian housing bubble has inflated the prices of Canadian banks' middle- and higher-income clients' homes; this in turn has allowed homeowners to take out huge lines of credit. Virtually everyone I know in Canada does not have a mortgage; they have lines of credit. They have been tapping into and refinancing these lines of credit as housing prices have exploded. Furthermore, it is estimated that over 100,000 Canadians in the Toronto area have multiple homes. Again, we witness the domino bottom-up effect of price decreases. Investors are unable to flip a home to buy two more homes or to get a mortgage for a new investment or rental property.

Equitable (EQB TSX)

Marc Cohodes, the famed short seller who exposed the FTX crypto fraud, has been on record saying, "Equitable will loan to anyone with a pulse." To heighten their revenue and size of their loan portfolio, Marc Cohodes stated, "If they could, they'd loan to dead people." In 2017 there was a debacle in a company called Home Capital Group (HCG) in Canada, which was bailed out by Warren Buffett, then ultimately taken private in 2023, which Mr. Cohodes predicted and made money shorting off. HCG in 2017 was on the verge of going under due to fraudulent loans. After the HCG debacle, Equitable received a $2 billion loan of their own. Since that 2017 bailout, Equitable's portfolio skyrocketed as they became more aggressive as HCG struggled to keep in business.

According to Marc Cohodes, regarding Equitable, "They have $1.2 billion of uninsured loan exposure in Alberta. That's 130% of book value. Raising loan-loss provisions by 160 basis points would wipe out one year's worth of the company's earnings."*

First National (FN TSX)

Many of the same individuals involved with Equitable are involved with First National. The stock did suffer losses when the HCG news became public. However, First National was able to bounce back in 2016 before being hit by the Covid crash. It is very hard to decipher financials with these large companies, as we really do not know the quality and perimeters of the loans. One should note that the company also has more than $100 billion in mortgages under administration—many of these would likely be defaulted on or underwater if there is a serious recession in Canadian housing prices. First National has also been very aggressive in building this portfolio in the recent bubble years of Canadian housing.

A STRATEGY TO PROSPER FROM THE POPPING OF THE EVERYTHING BUBBLE—OPTIONS STRADDLES

As I was writing this book, some bad news happened in terms of potential shorts. One of my favorite gauges of the market, Sotheby's, just was taken over by a private equity firm (the takeover itself is a sign of a bubble, as I will point out shortly).

Sotheby's is the internationally famous high-end real estate and auction firm. Sotheby's operates in the areas of high-end housing, car auctions, fine wine, and jewelry, all of which are sensitive to asset prices.

* From *The Globe and Mail*, October 2016, http://www.theglobeandmail.com/globe-investor/investment-ideas/high-profile-short-seller-takes-aim-at-5-canadian-companies/article32260555/.

As the Dow has soared from under 800 to north of 44,000 in the past 40-plus years, it helped support the art, wine, and collectibles market. Rich people own stocks, and they love to collect expensive things. When they make money in assets, the rich tend to spend it on art, fine wines, private planes, and so on. Sotheby's was a direct beneficiary of this.

Since going public in 1989, Sotheby's experienced three major boom-and-bust periods. The first was 1990, when Sotheby's fell from $16 a share to just above $4 when the Japanese stock market bubble burst (the Japanese were the largest buyers of art and high-end real estate during the eighties). In 1999, Sotheby's topped at around $37 per share, declining to $5 during the dot-com bust. Finally, in 2008, Sotheby's rallied to $46, crashing again to $5 during the financial crisis, before recovering to $60 during the everything bubble of the last 10 years.

In 2019, Sotheby's received a takeover offer from BidFair (owned by billionaire Patrick Drahi) for $3.7 billion, or $56 a share. Essentially, this is an effect of the everything bubble. The $3.7 billion price tag comes despite the material fact that Sotheby's revenues have been stuck around $1 billion over the past four years.

So with this leverage play on the everything bubble now gone, are there still macro ways to play and benefit from the bursting of the everything bubble?

I have a great strategy for the average investor to short the market and mitigate risk. This strategy is through what is known in the option world as *straddling*. A straddle is when you put both a call (a bet a company will go up in price) and a put (a bet it will go down in price). When you are using this strategy, you are just looking for a big move in either direction.

Jeff Gundlach, the famed bond manager, recently put such a trade on the TLT. His belief was that in early 2019, bonds would move big either way. The TLT, which tracks the 20-year bond in the

United States, had a huge move to the upside in 2019, trading up from $120 a share to over $132 (a 10% move in bond prices is a huge move in the government bond world). Mr. Gundlach's straddle paid off 22% in less than half a year, a massive return in the bond world where returns tend to be low.

The great thing about a straddle is it mitigates risk; you do not just need a market to fall or rise in a significant manner. So long as the price moves in one direction, you will make money.

For example, a stock I think is set up nicely for a straddle trade is Microsoft. Microsoft has been on fire recently, rising from just over $40 a share in 2015 to $460 as I write in 2024. When stocks get this hot and go parabolic, they usually continue the move or see a large correction.

A pure straddle is doing an option at the same price on either side of the trade at the price the stock is trading at. So let's look at the $460 January 2025 calls and puts on MSFT. The $460 calls trade around $34 and the $460 puts trade around $28 (the calls are more expensive because MSFT has been just going straight up for years, so that is where the money is being placed). Let's say MSFT moves $100 in each direction before January 2025. If MSFT trades down to $360, the puts go from $28 to $100, and if it goes to $560, from $34 to $100. One option in each would cost about $3,400 on the call side and $2,800 on the put side, so roughly $6,200. If it moves $100 in either direction, the trade would be worth $10,000, so you make roughly 65% on the trade. The key for a straddle like this is you need a large move in either direction. Therefore, if you are putting on such a trade, you need to believe the stock is going to have a big move, because if it has a small move, both sides of the trade will lose. But if there is a large move, you make more than owning the stock and are hedged in case of a decline!

Sotheby's was an example of a straddle trade that would have worked. In May, the January 2020 $33 puts were trading around $2 a share with the stock at $36, and the January 2020 $39 calls were roughly the same price (both $3 out of the money). When the stock was taken over for $56 a share, calls jumped to $17 a share, or an 8x return, totaling your return of four times on your money, with the put side of the straddle being worthless.

This is a fantastic way to play bubbles. If the everything bubble continues due to money printing to bail out the economy, stocks will go up and your calls should make you money. If the bubble bursts and there is some sort of bear market or crash, you will make money on the put side. All you need is a large move in either direction. If you are interested in such trades, my newsletter has such trades that are updated on a regular basis.

CONCLUSION

In this chapter we discussed the everything bubble, essentially the term that encompasses all the inflated assets worldwide.

- **U.S. Asset Bubble.** American U.S. equity valuation is near all-time highs. The market cap to GDP, price to sales, and CAPE ratio are all showing that we are nearing the extremes seen in 2000, 2020, and 2021, all of which lead to bear markets
- **Global Real Estate Bubble.** Real estate in the United States is unaffordable as ever, as prices spiked during the zero-rate era after Covid; now rates are much higher, but prices are not off by much. Canadian and Australian real estate are at nosebleed levels with their populations highly in debt. We have highlighted some of the Canadian

lenders we will be watching for the real estate bubble in Canada.

- **Shorting the Parabolic Curve.** We have also given you ways to short companies such as Nvidia in case the bubble bursts. All the signs are that the Magnificent Seven are hugely stretched in price and could fall hard in price. These stocks make up a larger percentage of the S&P 500 than any stocks ever had. This time of limited leadership tends to happen near the end of bull markets. There are numerous individual short-equity ETFs you can trade now to short these securities.
- **Option Strategies for the Bursting of the Everything Bubble.** We also gave you an everything bubble option strategy using straddles. If the everything bubble continues, certain stocks and sectors will continue to soar in price. However, if it bursts, these stocks will collapse. Using a straddle strategy will create a positive return either way. If there is a big reversal, stocks will fall and the put side of the trade will work. This is a great strategy for carefully investing in a bubble market that is bound to burst.

3

Hypernormalization: Shifting from Financial to Political Power

This chapter is named after a recent 2016 documentary by Adam Curtis, who works for BBC. It's a fascinating documentary regarding the history of the Western world dating back to the 1930s. You can find the documentary on YouTube, and I highly recommend it to anyone interested in the current political and economic environment.

THE SOVIET UNION EXPERIENCE AND HYPERNORMALIZATION

Hypernormalization was a term coined during the 1970s in the Soviet Union. Forget the propaganda you hear in the media or from Western governments; the Soviet citizens did not truly believe that they were still a great empire during the 1970s and 1980s. Truthfully, much like many of us in the West today, they realized that their economy was falling apart and was becoming stagnant. Also, like the West, their technocrats were trying to portray that everything was fine. However, even the average person was able to see the economy wasn't doing well, especially after a failed war in Afghanistan. Due to the government telling everyone that the economy was great, hypernormalization became the term for when the fake seemed real.

The problem with the Soviets was that they didn't know anything about any other economic system; they did not know if or when the fakeness would end. All they did know was that they couldn't conceive the system failing despite knowledge it clearly wasn't working.

For the last 20 years in the West, we haven't seen anything other than booms and busts, lurching from bubble to bubble. The common denominator was and has always been cheap money issued by central bankers, which was used to prop up debt and equity markets after massive drawdowns.

THE UNITED STATES AND HYPERNORMALIZATION

Since the bursting of the dot-com bubble, we have had two historically weak recoveries with wages stagnating. As we have discussed in prior chapters, central banks have taken advantage of cheap money to prop up asset markets while many people have fallen behind. Orwellian economic statistics are frequently resorted to. For example, those who are not in the labor force are not counted in the unemployment numbers; inflation numbers are forged to signal that things are OK.

Despite the apparently persuasive economic statistics, the average person looks around and sees that things aren't really that good; the cost of living is high, and health care and education costs are rising. Additionally, we must work longer for less (the biggest rise in the participation rate in the labor force is people over 65, as they must continue to work in retirement to survive). Therefore, we have our own form of hypernormalization in the Western world.

The proof is in the pudding; the reason that "populists" have won in places like Italy and the United States, and the reason they poll strongly in France and the United Kingdom (winning the Brexit vote), is because people subconsciously recognize the economic fallout despite the statistics showing them something else. This all came to a head during the Covid-19 lockdown when violent protests broke out after the killing of George Floyd.

The protests were not just about race, but rather an undertone that something was wrong with the system. As we discussed previously, we have seen numerous pandemics in the last 100 years: the 1957 Asian flu, 1968 Hong Kong flu, and even the 2009 swine flu; however, none of them sank the economy. Even the infamous 1918 Spanish flu, which was the worst pandemic since the Middle Ages, did not cause the economy to enter a recession. The mere fact that the economy shut down for a few weeks revealed the true issues that our modern society is facing; too many individuals and corporations alike are living paycheck to paycheck.

Now, what does this have to do with financial markets? If you go to a city like London or New York, you will see buildings with million-dollar apartments that foreign investors own but nobody lives in. Much of the buying in the recovery after the financial crisis was not just rich foreigners, but also wealth management companies buying empty apartments, then turning around and renting them out and receiving return on equity from the rental income. Thus, there really hasn't been a rebound in home ownership during the recovery in the United States, as home ownership levels are still near multi-decade lows.

Because of quantitative easing, countries with very weak economies and high debt levels (such as Italy and Spain) had long-term interest rates of under 3% until 2022. At the peak of the bond market in the summer of 2020, nearly $21 trillion in bonds worldwide were trading with negative yields! We view these extremes in interest rates as normal due to central bank intervention.

If you look at how markets traded from 2012 to 2019, there was virtually no volatility, and going almost straight up, this was hypernormal: printed money has helped squash market volatility and created all sorts of bubbles, as was discussed in Chapter 2. We have seen companies using more money than they have in cash flow, to buy back stock. As stated in Chapter 1, the government is funding most of these buybacks as the interest rates on borrowed money are so low. Now we view the huge growth in corporate debt and excessive buyback programs as normal. However, historically, this has not been the norm; cheap money has created a fake or hypernormal market bubble, or the everything bubble, where we now view these extreme tactics as normal.

The first crack of financial hypernormalization was the blowback from the housing and leverage bubble during the financial crisis. The next crack will be when the corporate debt bubble and potentially government debt bubble burst. Put simply, when both debt bubbles burst, cheap money and debt can no longer drive growth and the equity markets.

Again, like the Soviet Union in 1991, we are about to see the end of our hypernormalized financial markets. The Brexit vote in the United Kingdom and the election of Donald Trump in the United States are signs that, like the technocrats of the Soviet Union, the technocrats of our central banks and governments have once again failed. Like the citizens in the Soviet Union, we now realize that our system of so-called neoliberalism has failed. Although the solutions to this failure differ in nature on both the left and right, both are equally as culpable. These being printing money, as well as government's spending money on the left or on the right to support large corporations that just "use" the system to their advantage through stock buybacks and lobbying, giving nothing back to society.

I listen to a lot of podcasts while I work and write. One political commentator I listen to is Tim Pool, who frequently discusses the various biases of the media. In one recent podcast, Tim discussed why poverty and homelessness are so high in places like San Francisco and Los Angeles despite the supposed booming of these cities. Tim notes that while the economy is doing well in these places, especially San Francisco where a new tech boom has created wealth, the cost of living is out of control. Due to these high costs, since 2022 California has seen a net outflow of people for the first time in its history.

Where I am from in Canada, specifically Ontario, housing prices have boomed. The average price of a house in Toronto is near what it is in Manhattan and San Francisco. Prepandemic unemployment was at multi-decade lows. When I would go back from the Bahamas (where I now live) and visit, I found it difficult to find the feeling and aura of prosperity. Housing is so expensive that most people are living paycheck to paycheck just to pay their mortgages. The population has increased so heavily that roads are overcrowded and overcongested. Approximately 45% of Canadians are $200 away from not being able to pay their bills. When the pandemic hit, almost a quarter of Canadians were in danger of missing mortgage payments, with nearly half of the homeowners in Vancouver in danger.

I feel these are two perfect examples of hypernormalization. Despite a supposed boom, day-to-day life is worse for many people. The cheap money that has led to these stock market and housing price booms is masking the fact that the quality of everyday life is declining for many people.

Central bankers can no longer continue to tell us that everything is fine when we see popular uprisings. Conclusively, I believe we are about to go through a period where power is going to shift from the central bankers and financial engineers back to politicians.

POWER SHIFTS

In the last 90 years, there were two major geopolitical and economic power shifts. The first shift was in the 1930s when the world moved from financial and economic power to political power under Roosevelt. Roosevelt increased regulation on financial firms and started a government infrastructure stimulus program, effectively instituting the first modern-day welfare programs. In a show of power, he was one of the first presidents to throw Wall Street bankers in jail. He showed that politicians could be a force in the economy and in day-to-day life.

The second shift began with the end of the gold standard in 1972 and the oil embargo in 1974. When the United States went off the gold standard, it made money much looser and created more boom-and-bust cycles, thus increasing speculation and the influence financial markets had on the oil economy. This was all fed by oil money. The oil embargo, which caused oil prices to spike, caused a huge amount of petrodollar money to flow to the Middle East oil barons. The oil barons then gave the money to western bankers who speculated all over the world with it. This helped cause a boom and bust in South America and increasingly gave bankers more power due to their access to ever-increasing amounts of Middle East money.

This shift then sped up under Reagan and Thatcher. Both deregulated and cut taxes in their economies. In each nation, the power shifted from the industrialized sectors of the economy to the financial sector; geographic shifts transferred power from the industrialized areas and cities into the financial centers of New York and London.

The extent of this financial power probably peaked during the housing bubble of the mid-2000s and then ended decisively during the financial crisis of 2008, when politicians had to come to rescue the bankers. The bailouts and quantitative easing (QE) are an attempt to keep the power in the world financial markets, but it is fake. Financially engineered hypernormalization has failed; we have the everything bubble, but no one really believes things are better. The shift to political power now seems to be completing itself with the Brexit vote and the election of Donald Trump.

In each of the last two shifts, a major financial crisis followed. The 1970s' oil embargo, high inflation, and high unemployment have led to deregulation and the movement away from government power. The 1929 crash and the Great Depression led to Roosevelt and politicians gaining more power. Therefore, I expect a crash sometime within the next few years, with the end of the everything bubble giving more power to Trump and other populists.

A large crash in the stock market and/or a recession will probably speed up the power shift back to politicians and away from central banks, as the central bankers will be blamed (rightfully so) for this bubble and crash. Now is the time to prepare for the end of the hypernormalization of financial markets and prepare for a new normal. Chapters 1 and 2 introduced ways to potentially make money when these hypernormalization or cheap money bubbles pop. The following sections discuss what we see as the major shifts and the next potential booms after these bubbles burst.

FROM HYPERNORMALIZATION TO QE FOR THE PEOPLE

The boom of the last 10 years has been mostly restricted to financial assets. When the Fed and other central banks started QE, many, including myself, expected to see some sort of inflation. However, inflation at the consumer level (price inflation) has been tame, whereas inflation in asset markets (stocks, bonds, etc.) has been fierce. Why is this?

The answer is simply because this QE was targeted at risk taking and asset markets. When markets collapsed in 2008, the Fed began to buy mortgage-backed securities and government bonds. They bought mortgage-backed securities to stabilize the housing markets, and they bought government bonds so people wouldn't just park their money in bonds instead of taking risk. The Trouble Asset Relief Program (TARP) gave $700 billion to the banks to shore up the balance sheet, encouraging banks not to be afraid to lend to each other.

One of the issues during the Great Depression was no one knew which bank was safe to keep their money! Thus, banks were scared to lend to each other and many of them failed. As banks failed, people became more insecure when it came to storing money in banks. This was predigital money, so people were doing things as simple as buying gold coins (before gold became illegal to own in 1933) or just keeping their cash in a box under their bed mattress! As lending is backed by deposits, when deposits disappeared, even more banks went under, causing a domino effect. Hence, the rationale of TARP to keep banks adequately capitalized.

However, you must look at where this money flowed after TARP and the QE. A lot of it sat in excess reserve accounts, meaning it never flowed into the economy.

Velocity is a great indicator to back this theory; the velocity of money is a measure of how fast money passes from one holder to the next. It is most commonly measured as the income velocity of money, which is the frequency at which the average unit of currency is used to purchase newly domestically produced goods and services within a given time period. Currently, the velocity of money, which peaked during the late 1990s, is near 100-year lows! This means money is not passing from one person to the next, and not rotating into the real economy.

All this money has gone into the financial markets. If you make money cheap by purchasing bonds and by chasing institutions out of the bond market by making them look for yield, they are going to speculate for returns. This means that money will stay in the financial markets. These institutions will loan it to corporations, or even speculate in stocks or venture capital.

As most of these assets are owned by the rich, they will then use this money to buy other assets: real estate, art, stocks, private planes, and so on. Rich people don't need money to buy basic goods.

This is something I fully admit I got wrong. When the Fed began QE in 2009, I thought it would cause huge inflation like the printing of money in Venezuela or Argentina. However, as there is no velocity of money, most of the money is going into asset markets and not the real economy.

However, I think that when the current bubble bursts, we will see the end of this financial hypernormalization where asset prices only went up and few people benefited. The next round of QE will go into the economy. Debt is also now so much higher than it was in 2009. I think this debt will have to be inflated away and again cause much higher inflation in the real economy than in the 2010s.

One of the shifts I think we will see after the next bust will be a move back to political power. In the 1920s, Calvin Coolidge, the laissez-faire Republican president of the time, was famous for saying that the "business of America is business." After the crash, a lot of the leverage and corruption in the economy was exposed. Roosevelt moved power back to the political power realm. He started the U.S. Securities and Exchange Commission (SEC) and other government agencies to bolster the regulation in America, including the New Deal, a huge stimulus project aimed at bringing the economy out of the Depression.

Just like the 1920s and the 2010s and early 2020s, SAS* financial and technology companies drive growth. The stock market has boomed, as did Silicon Valley.

---

* SAS is a statistical software suite used in financial companies for data management, analytics, and more. SAS software uses artificial intelligence, machine learning, and deep learning to model and manage data. SAS Regulatory Capital Management is an SAS software solution that helps financial institutions manage regulatory capital calculation and reporting.

One of the aspects driving people toward populist movements, be it on the left or right, is that these cheap money policies have only really benefited the elites. What's interesting is that both Donald Trump, a right-wing populist, and Jeremy Corbyn, the former left-wing leader of the Labour Party in the United Kingdom, called for massive infrastructure projects. Corbyn called it "QE for the people." Having seen how successful QE was in inflating asset prices, his argument is that the next round should be used to build roads, schools, and so on. Corbyn's plan was for a government-run bank, called the National Investment Bank, to issue bonds. The central bank would buy them, and then the proceeds of those bonds would be used for the government stimulus program.

Another policy of "QE for the people" will be universal basic income (UBI). UBI is just what it sounds like; it's a sum of money paid out by the government per month to every qualified individual in the country. UBI is supported by Andrew Yang and many other Democratic politicians. The main theory behind it is that it gives a basic standard of living to everyone in the country. The idea is to subsidize and help those who are dislocated by job loss due to technological advances, or those who are in school and having difficulty maintaining a living wage.

Many who support a universal basic income want it in the range of $1,000 to $1,500 a month. There are variances on the program. For example, Yang is a moderate who wants the income so in turn you do not have to raise the minimum wage. It essentially subsidizes small businesses that cannot afford a $15 to $20 or higher minimum wage. More extreme proponents support its implementation plus an increase in minimum wages and other social programs. Recent polls show that roughly 50% of Americans support UBI.

Let me state that just by talking about these policies, I do not intend to mean that I support them. I am simply showing the details of some of these proposals. If something like a UBI is introduced, it will be a form of "QE for the people." Instead of money going to banks or into financial institutions, it will go directly into people's bank accounts.

UBI would, however, be very costly. According to Ray Dalio, the former manager of Bridgewater Associates, the largest hedge fund in the world, the estimated cost to give every American citizen $12,000 per year, given the current poverty threshold, would be roughly $3.8 trillion annually. The figure represents 17% of the U.S. GDP and 70% of tax revenue. Some existing welfare programs probably could be eliminated and replaced by the UBI, but these welfare programs account for only a small portion of the budget (less than $1 trillion a year). Additionally, those collecting Social Security would probably not be eligible for this, as they are receiving a pension. However, just the raw estimate alone shows you how expensive this program is, and I am sure a large part of it would be funded by QE or money printing.

Another form of "QE for the people" is a monetary movement called modern monetary theory (MMT). In a nutshell, MMT works under the premise that the debts issued in your own currency cannot be defaulted; therefore, a nation can print money to buy the debt and issue it for government projects, spending, and so on. In fact, the Green New Deal, which is estimated to cost trillions of dollars, would mostly be funded by MMT. Be it UBI, universal health care, or infrastructure programs, they will all get paid for by MMT.

With the disillusionment on both sides of the political spectrum should there be another downturn in the economy, the next form of QE is not going to be buying up assets and reinflating stock, real estate, and other markets to benefit the rich. Corbyn in the United Kingdom wanted "QE for the people"; leftists in the United States who support the Green New Deal want some form of MMT to fund their huge program. Even Trump on the right would like to do some sort of large infrastructure project. Therefore, I firmly believe that the next round of money printing will not go directly into bank vaults and financial markets; this round will go into some sort of "QE for the people," be it infrastructure, UBI, or the Green New Deal, and so on.

If this sort of stimulus occurs, it will increase the velocity of money, and demand for real goods will soar. This will be inflationary. In such an inflationary environment, gold and silver, base metals, and mining stocks will perform very well. The first part of this chapter laid out the hypernormalization economy, why it will end, and why the shift to political willpower will lead to "QE for the people." The next part of the chapter will discuss certain commodities that will benefit from this potential shift and a stimulus that goes into the real economy.

COMMODITIES

Precious Metals—Gold and Silver

It seems that in all my books, I am writing about gold and silver. Believe it or not, I am not a gold bug. (A gold bug is always bullish on gold.) However, my feeling since the late 1990s is that we are in a super cycle bull market for gold that could last decades, and I still feel this is the case.

Why a Gold Bull Market?

Before delving into gold and gold investments, let's quickly go over why gold is considered a currency of its own.

Due to the metallurgical makeup of gold, it does not disintegrate or rust. It essentially has lasted "forever" in roughly 10,000 years in human history. As there is a relatively finite supply globally, gold obviously cannot be printed or devalued (if the price goes too high, more will be mined, causing an oversupply, with gold falling in value). However, a mining boom would take literally years to unfold, as gold is hard to find and supply tends to be steady.

Currencies have come and gone; coins were used in ancient Rome but devalued to almost worthless as the Roman empire expanded and bankrupted itself. No one uses Roman coins anymore to buy goods and services (even the empire itself had 12 different types of coins, which changed over hundreds of years). Then the Ottoman empire, Austro-Hungarian empire, French empire, Spanish empire, Soviet empire, British and American empires—all except the British and Americans have experienced either a collapse of their currency or some form of hyperinflation. However, even the British and American currencies both have lost more than 95% of their value due to inflation over the past 100-plus years.

If you adjust gold's price for inflation, it has kept its value for hundreds and even thousands of years, while these fiat currencies have come and gone.

Returns of Gold

When purchasing gold, like with any asset, you want to wait and purchase it when it's cheap. Over the long term, gold keeps up relatively well with inflation. However, if you buy at the right time, its returns can significantly outperform other asset classes. Tables 3.1 and 3.2 give the returns for gold and the S&P 500 for the last 20 years as of mid-2019 (the latest numbers I could find).

TABLE 3.1 Gold annualized returns for 20 years as of 2019

1-yr: –1.5%	6-yr: –1.3%	11-yr: 3.1%	16-yr: 8.1%
2-yr: 1.3%	7-yr: –2.7%	12-yr: 5.8%	17-yr: 8.5%
3-yr: 1.6%	8-yr: –2.1%	13-yr: 5.5%	18-yr: 8.8%
4-yr: 1.6%	9-yr: 0.8%	14-yr: 8.4%	19-yr: 8.5%
5-yr: –0.1%	10-yr: 3.1%	15-yr: 8.4%	20-yr: 8.1%

TABLE 3.2 S&P 500 annualized total returns as of 2019

1-yr: 5.2%	6-yr: 11.5%	11-yr: 8.8%	16-yr: 9.3%
2-yr: 10.5%	7-yr: 13.7%	12-yr: 7.5%	17-yr: 7.8%
3-yr: 13.4%	8-yr: 12.2%	13-yr: 8.6%	18-yr: 6.5%
4-yr: 9.4%	9-yr: 13.4%	14-yr: 8.5%	19-yr: 5.8%
5-yr: 10.4%	10-yr: 14.5%	15-yr: 8.7%	20-yr: 5.8%

These two tables show the annualized returns for gold and for stocks via the S&P 500 over the 20 years from 2000 to 2019. In the 10 years that followed the 2009 stock market bottom from 2009 to 2019, the S&P had an annualized return of 14.5%, whereas gold had a return of only 3.1% (in 2009 gold was 9 years into an 11-year bull market). This shows you the importance of *when* and what levels you buy at, which we will discuss later in the chapters on maximum pessimism.

While it is impossible to time markets exactly, these tables show why you must try to at least buy when one asset is cheap and not buy when they are expensive. Earlier in this book, we discovered that in the late 1990s, stocks as per virtually every valuation measure (market cap to GDP, price to sales, price to earning, etc.) were expensive. If you had purchased during the late 1990s or in 2000 when these valuations were high, the returns have been extremely mediocre (roughly 5.8% a year over 20 years). Comparatively, if you purchased stocks in 2008 and 2009 when they had cheaper historical valuations, the annualized returns jumped to 14.5% and 13.4%.

From 1998 to 2004, when gold was cheap compared to stocks (gold had been in a near 20-year bear market, falling from $850 in 1980 to near $250 in 2001), returns have been better than the S&P 500 during this time to the present. However, after gold soared nearly 700% to $1,900 an ounce in 2011, gold was obviously no longer cheap, and the returns in gold from 2011 to 2019 were mediocre. (See Figure 3.1.)

FIGURE 3.1 Gold–to–S&P 500 ratio.
Source: www.stockcharts.com

WHERE DO WE STAND NOW?

Nowadays, gold is cheap when compared to equities. A simple way of measuring gold's valuation in comparison to equities is simply taking the price of gold and dividing it by the price of the S&P 500. This is the number of shares of the S&P 500 it takes to buy one ounce of gold.

When the ratio of gold to the S&P is 2 to 1, it means that gold is expensive and the S&P is cheap. When it takes less than half of an ounce of gold to buy the S&P, it means that the S&P is expensive and gold is cheap. For example, in 1980 gold was 800 and the S&P was 100, so the ratio was 8 to 1; the S&P rallied to 1,500 over the next 20 years and gold fell more than 60% for 20 years! In 2000 gold was $300 and the S&P was 1,500, so the ratio was 0.20. Gold rallied to $1,900 over the next 11 years and the S&P fell 20%! At the moment, the S&P is about 6,000 as I write and gold is $2,700 an ounce, meaning that gold is less than half the price of the S&P 500 and cheap!

In the mid-1960s, gold was trading at $35 an ounce and the S&P climbed to near 100, meaning gold was less than half the price of the S&P. From the mid-1960s to 1980, gold soared from $35 to

$850 an ounce, while the S&P remained flat from 1966 to 1982. This indicator really blew off in the late 1990s and 2000 when gold traded at 1/6th the price of the S&P 500. After this extreme reading, gold traded from roughly $250 to nearly $1,900 and the S&P topped at over 1,500 in 2000, bottoming at 666 in 2009! The S&P did not break above its year 2000 high until 2013.

On the flip side, the gold–to–S&P 500 ratio traded up to 4 to 1 in the 1930s and 1940s and again in 1980. This means it took four shares of the S&P 500 to buy one ounce of gold, rather than taking multiple ounces of gold to buy one share of the S&P 500. In the 1940s, gold did nothing for the next 20-plus years (remember, it was locked in price at $35 an ounce). The S&P 500, on the other hand, bottomed at 9 in 1942 and soared to over 100 by the late 1960s!

This is a long-term indicator and not going to time markets over the short term, meaning it could take years for the long-term reversal to occur. However, if you start buying gold or stocks when the ratio hits extremes, it works over a 10-to-15-year period.

If you bought gold and gold equities in the early to mid-1960s, or in the late 1990s, the S&P 500 clearly outperformed. However, over the next 10 years, gold and gold equities did much better than the S&P 500. Vice versa for purchasing the S&P 500 when it was cheap compared to gold.

In 2010 the gold–to–S&P 500 ratio traded above 1.50 after reaching a record low of 0.25 in the late 1990s. As I write in 2024, the ratio is 0.46, meaning that the S&P is trading at over twice the price of gold and gold is cheap compared to the S&P.

I believe we are seeing something like the 1961–1980 bull market in gold equities (this cycle is just taking longer). Gold bullion itself did not begin to climb until 1973, because its price was fixed. However, gold equities began to climb in 1961, in a de facto increase in the price of gold.

During the 1961 bull market, there were two major moves: the first was from 1961 to 1974 when gold came off its lows and became an inflationary hedge during the Vietnam War and during the Middle East oil embargo of 1974. This move saw the price of gold climb from the fixed price of $35 an ounce to nearly $200, and the Barron's gold stock index (the major index of the time) climbed from roughly 30 to over 500! Following the rally, there was a roughly 18-month bear market where gold fell nearly 50% in price to $104 an ounce. Naturally, the Barron's gold stock index also fell nearly 60% from 500 to 200. In the second move, from 1976 to 1980, gold climbed from $104 to $850 an ounce, with the Barron's gold stock index going from 200 to over 1,000.

The current cycle, which began in 2000, had an 11-year upward move into 2011, followed by a nearly 4-year bear market into 2015, then rallied off the lows in 2016 and a consolidation since that time. Gold has broken out to new highs in 2024, and I feel the gold equities will follow in the coming years.

The Longer the Base, the Bigger the Space

When we look at Figure 3.2, we see that there was a near 6-year base in gold from 2013 to 2019, ranging between $1,050 on the downside and $1,380 on the upside. In technical analysis, there is a simple saying that "the longer the base, the more the space." This simply means that the longer a stock or commodity spends going sideways, the larger and longer the upside break usually is. We saw this in gold back in the 1990s: all throughout the decade, gold had been between $250 and $450 an ounce. When it finally did break out in 2003, gold soared to nearly $1,900 an ounce.

Gold just broke through this base and is trading over $2,600 an ounce as I write. I suspect this is the start of a much larger move to the upside.

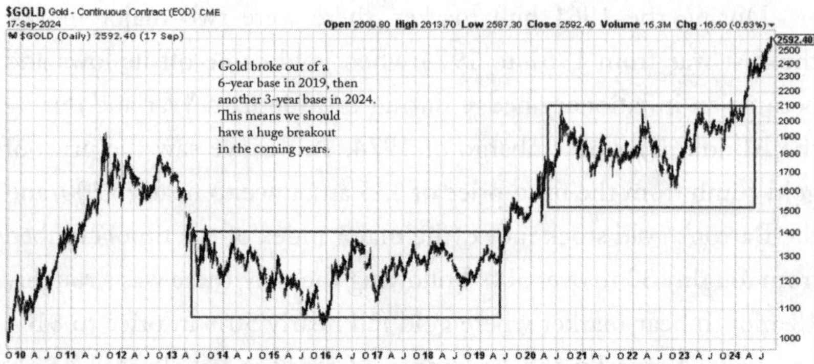

FIGURE 3.2 Gold: The longer the base, the more the space.
Source: www.stockcharts.com

What will the catalyst be? Probably a decline in the stock market. When that occurs, the Federal Reserve will be forced to reverse course and cut interest rates to add liquidity like they did in 2001 and 2009 when gold soared. Even the 2020–2021 period saw gold trade very strong as the Fed cut rates and printed money. Also, we have the added tailwind of a super-high debt level, which is leading many large investors into gold, as they fear some sort of debt crisis in the coming years.

Another catalyst will be the interest rate cuts that should begin in late 2024 and into 2025. I have done a lot of extensive research on this, which I will talk about in the gold stock section. When the Fed begins and continues a rate cut cycle, gold equities are about the strongest-performing sector of the stock market, as we will show.

I believe the gold market is like the 1999–2001 period, more than the 2007–2008 period. In 2008 gold and gold stocks crashed with the markets, but part of the reason they did was because gold and gold stocks climbed with the market from 2002 to 2007. Therefore, investors, funds, and so on were "gold-long" and on gold equities. When the market fell, they had to liquidate gold and gold equities just like they had to sell everything else.

However, during the 1999–2001 period, gold had been in a cyclical bear market since 1996. Longer term it was completing a secular bear market that it had been in since 1980. This made gold and gold equities cheap, beaten up, and underowned. It also is why gold and gold stocks climbed in price from 2000 to 2002, even as the market fell. Even though gold bullion has broken out to new highs in 2024, gold equities remain in a bear market, with most having fallen 40–50% or more from their 2011 highs. Like the 2000 period, gold and gold equities are underowned. I expect that once the market declines again, gold stocks will rally, counter to the market, then crash with it like 2008.

Gold Equities

Gold equities are obviously much different than gold. The 20-year returns on gold are roughly 9% a year; even since the peak in 2011, the average annualized return is only slightly negative (roughly negative 2% a year). Additionally, stocks have vastly underperformed, falling over 80% from their 2011 highs to 2015 lows, and they are still about 65% below these highs as I write in 2024.

With gold and gold stocks, you have many variables that factor into the price, movement, and valuation.

The first is total production of gold. A gold company produces only so many ounces a year; this can go down if prices fall and the cost of production is no longer profitable. It's not just like producing iPhones or cars, where the more the demand, the more you make. Gold is finite. To replenish these ounces, you usually must (1) drill the property further, (2) find new properties to replace ounces, or (3) take over other companies who possess mines and fund the production. All three of these are a costly process.

One of the intricacies of production is so many things can go wrong at a mine. You can have an accident at the mine, political problems in higher-risk countries, issues with environmental permitting, and so on.

Gold Stocks as an Example of the Cheap Money Bubble

When gold rose from 2001 to 2011, the sector had access to cheap money like most other sectors. The access to cheap capital caused a huge misallocation of capital and is a warning to other sectors as to what can happen when cheap money is misallocated. When gold was high and money was cheap, large companies took on billions in debt to take over mines and expand production.

Companies and properties that were taken over at near $1,900 an ounce were nowhere near as profitable under $1,300 an ounce. Companies that did the takeovers had to divest of higher-cost properties and write down values. Many of the same companies that were taking on debt to go on a takeover splurge from 2005 to 2011 are now paying off that debt (we will have more on that when we discuss individual companies). This is one reason why gold equities so vastly underperformed gold during this decline. Gold fell about 45% from top to bottom, but the equities fell more than 80%!

Gold equities usually have higher betas than gold, meaning they go up and down more than the price of the metal itself. This recent decline was made worse by the misallocation of capital, which was exacerbated by cheap money that was also available at the top of the market. If you look at the Barron's gold stock index, as we mentioned before, it nearly went back to its 2000 lows in 2015, even though gold was nearly four times higher than it was in 2000 than in 2015!

Gold Equities Are Trades, Not Long Long-Term Investments

Due to the volatile nature of gold stocks, they are not buy-and-hold investments. You want to buy them when they are undervalued and sell them into strength more so than almost any other asset class, due to their volatile nature. Despite the problems, they are worth investing in because they have so much profitability during bull markets in gold.

Figure 3.3 is a chart of the Barron's gold index, discussed in this chapter. This index has been in a huge trading range in the last 40-plus years. Despite gold moving from $100 to as high as $2,700 in the past 45 years, the Barron's gold stock index has traded in a wide range of 200 to over 1,600. Whenever it traded over 1,000 (1980, 1983, 1987, 2008, 2011), you wanted to sell into that strength, with bear markets of 50% or more following. Whereas readings under 500 in 1976, 1982, 1986, late 1990s, and 2008 were all great times to buy gold stocks, with rallies in the hundreds of percent following. The Barron's index is again trading under the 1,000 level as I write in 2024, telling us that they are again in the buy range, especially with gold trading at $2,600.

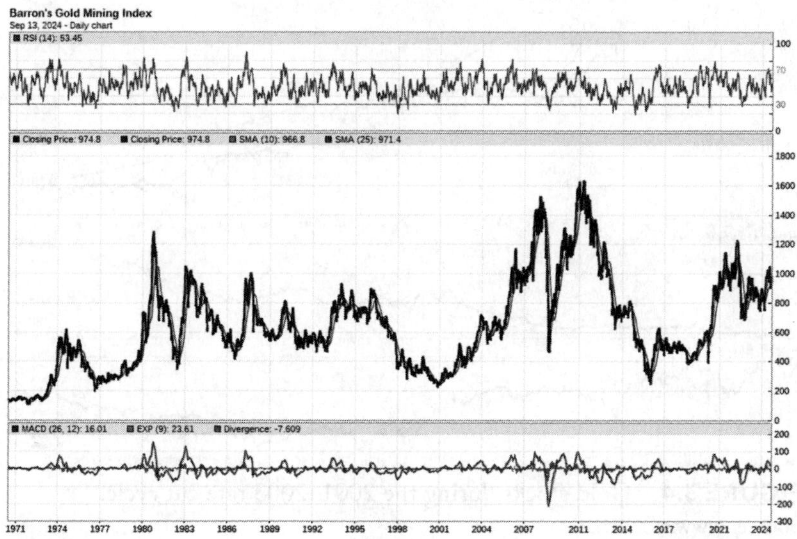

FIGURE 3.3 Barron's gold stock index.
Source: http://www.goldchartsrus.com/chartstemp/free/fchart-BGMI.php

In addition, during rate cut cycles, gold stocks perform very well. They are about the best-performing sector in the market. Figures 3.4, 3.5, and 3.6 show how gold and gold stocks performed during the rate cut cycles of 2001 to 2003, 2008 to 2011, and 2019 to 2020. You can see in each case gold stocks soared even during bear markets (in 2008 and 2020 gold stocks were hit during sell-offs, but were the first sector to reach new highs afterward). In the following figures, we show the 90-day Treasury bond yield (which tracks the Fed funds rate) with the performance of gold, gold stocks, and the S&P 500 during these rate cut cycles.

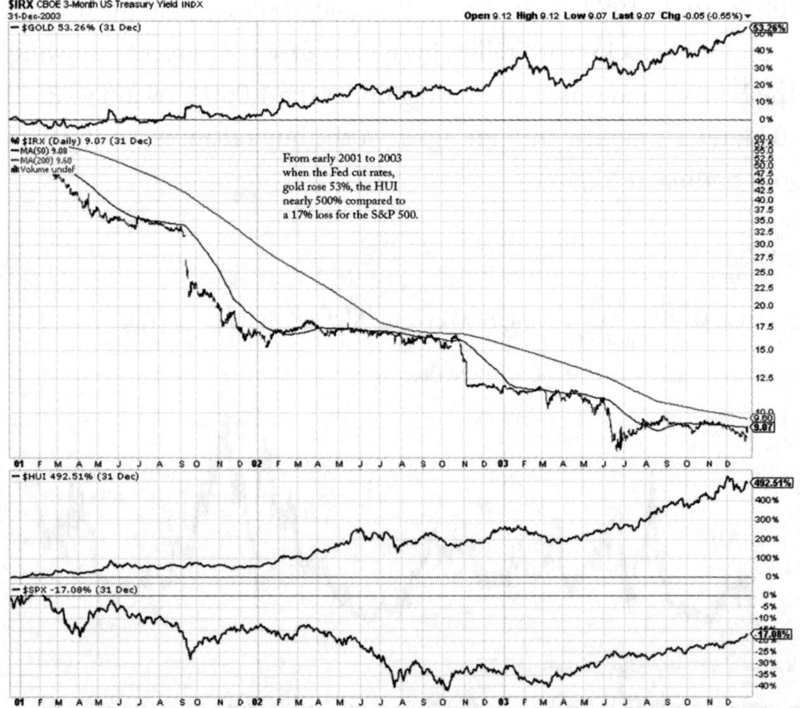

FIGURE 3.4 Gold stocks during the 2001–2003 rate cut cycle.
Source: www.stockcharts.com

FIGURE 3.5 Gold stocks during the 2008–2011 rate cut cycle.
Source: www.stockcharts.com

FIGURE 3.6 Gold stocks during the 2019–2020 rate cut cycle.
Source: www.stockcharts.com

As you can see in all three of these rate cut cycles, in the first one to three years of the cycle from 2001 to 2003, 2008 to 2011, and 2019 to 2020, gold equities vastly outperformed the S&P 500. From 2001 to 2003, the HUI Gold Bugs Index ($HUI) gained almost 500%, whereas the S&P 500 fell 17%. After the crash of 2008 when the Fed cut rates to zero, gold equities rallied over 160% into 2011, whereas the S&P rose 26%. Finally, the rate cut cycle began in 2019 just before the Covid crash of 2020. From mid-2019 to the summer of 2020 during the first year of the rate cut cycle, gold equities rose over 100%, whereas the S&P only rose 21%.

It should be noted that as bull markets mature, gold stocks tend to underperform. I believe the reason for this is because as the bull market and economic expansion mature, investors become more aggressive and want growth. So they will look to crypto, tech stocks, housing, and so on, more speculative forms of investing, and shun gold, and gold tends to underperform as the economy booms.

This book will be published in January 2025, and the Fed has just begun a rate cut cycle in September 2024 as I write, which should bode well for gold and gold stocks in 2025 and 2026.

HOW TO INVEST IN GOLD

In our final part on investing in gold, we will look at simple things that average investors can do themselves and how they can buy gold stocks. We will be looking at the various types of gold stocks and recommendations in funds and individual securities.

Gold Bullion and ETFs

If you are a conservative investor, the easiest way to invest in the gold market is just buying the metal. The metal doesn't have the huge volatility stocks have, and its performance holds up versus inflation and the stock market over a long-term period of time. In addition, as gold is trading more like how it traded in the 1990s and early 2000s (i.e., opposite to the stock market), gold should rise in a flight to safety.

If you want to buy the physical metal, there are dealers all over the United States and Canada. You can even buy the coins directly from the Canadian or American mint, as most of them make so many coins and bars every year. You must be a bit careful, as some of these dealers mark up prices and the industry does attract some shady people. When buying physical bullion, you must do your due diligence. For the sake of this book, I am going to concentrate on how to buy gold on the financial markets and not the physical.

The easiest way to buy the metal is through the SPDR Gold Sharers ETF GLD NYSE. This is a heavily traded ETF that trades on the New York Stock Exchange (NYSE). It owns gold certificates, and as the fund sees increases in inflows, it purchases more gold, and so on. This is a simple way for the average investor to own gold in a 401(k) or brokerage account.

The best way to own gold bullion in a fund is through the Sprott Physical Gold and Silver Trust (CEF) NYSE. What is interesting about this fund is that it is not an ETF but rather a closed-end investment fund that holds physical gold and silver. One of the major differences between an ETF and a closed-end fund is that an ETF tends to trade near its net asset value, while a closed-end fund can trade at a large premium or discount to the net asset value. As I write, the CEF is trading at a discount to the net asset value, which is incredible, as gold is trading near all-time highs. The CEF also has about 20% of its funds invested in silver, so it gives you exposure to silver as well.

Gold Equities

There are numerous ways to buy gold equities. Not only that, but within the gold equity sector, there are different forms of companies. The easiest way for investors to buy gold equities is through gold ETFs. Within the gold equities market, there are three different types of equities: (1) large-cap producers, which are the types of gold equities that trade on the NYSE; (2) mid-tier producers, which are smaller producers that usually have one or two mines and mainly trade on the TSE or in New York; and (3) junior exploration equities, which are smaller companies that are drilling for gold or about to go into production. These tend to trade on the TSX and CSE in Canada.

Gold Equity ETFs

Let's begin with the gold equity ETFs. The two major ETFs are the Van Eck Gold Miners ETF GDX NYSE and the Van Eck Junior Gold Miners ETF GDXJ NYSE. The GDX is an ETF of large-cap gold miners. It owns large-cap companies such as Barrick Gold and Newmont, and so on. The GDXJ owns mid-cap and smaller companies.

In the section on passive investing, I noted the problem with passive investing: when everyone owns ETFs, when they must sell the ETF, the ETF must sell the stocks that it owns, which causes the entire sector or market to fall. This happened in gold equities and the liquidation of gold equity ETFs, which helped push down the price of gold stocks a great deal.

The reverse is true after a crash or bear market. When the market turns around, individual investors and corporate investors will begin buying ETFs again. This means the ETF will have inflows and then will purchase these securities, which will then drive them higher. So while ETFs selling can cause bear markets to overshoot to the downside, they can also cause the market to rebound quicker as the money flows from the ETFs into the equities.

When gold topped in 2011, the GLD ETF held nearly 45 million ounces of gold. However, as gold sold out from 2011 to 2015, this decreased to only 20 million ounces. The bear market became a self-fulfilling prophecy. As prices continued to trade lower, investors sold and the ETF had to, in turn, sell more gold, which forced the price even lower.

Just as the ETF overowned gold in 2011, it underowned it at the bottom in 2015. When gold prices began to turn up higher, money flowed into the ETF, which bought gold and then helped push prices higher.

It should be noted that the ownership of the GLD ETF was so ridiculous at the top of the gold market in 2011 that the GLD had a larger market cap than the SPY, the S&P 500 ETF! This was a contrarian warning sign that the bull market in gold was overdone and gold was due for a correction. This is no longer the case, with the SPY now possessing net assets of nearly $566 billion and the GLD possessing assets as low as $69 billion in 2024, meaning the SPY now has over eight times the assets of the GLD. This may be another example of how underowned gold was compared to the stock market.

The forced liquidation of the ETFs was an even bigger issue in gold equity ETFs. Gold equities are much smaller than the companies listed in the S&P 500. When the bear market accelerated and investors piled out of the GDX and GDXJ, they then had to liquidate the equities that they owned, and as these companies are so small, it crushed them on the way down. In Chapter 7 on crypto, I will discuss how Bitcoin bulls should be careful that the Bitcoin does not do the same thing to bitcoin.

Much like the GLD, the GDX and GDXJ are now oversold and underowned; hence, what worked against them in the bear market can now work for them in the bull market. As gold and gold stocks move higher, inflows will come into these ETFs and the ETFs will have purchased more of the equities, which will push up prices.

The GDX currently only has a market cap of $13 billion, and the GDXJ is only $5 billion. Imagine if these two ETFs see tens of billions in inflows as gold prices and gold equities rise in price; this will cause an explosion of buying in gold equities. These two ETFs, which own dozens of gold equities, are the easiest way for the average investor to own a basket of equities in the sector.

Individual Gold Equities

For those of you who are interested in owning individual stocks, this book will cover two of the three gold-mining equity sectors. These being the large-cap and mid-tier sectors. We will go over what we believe makes up a good junior mining company, but we will not recommend any junior mining companies in this book, as they are too small in nature and much more time sensitive in terms of when and what to buy, which makes them unsuitable for a book.

Large-Cap Gold Equities. These are the big producers. Most of these stocks have been very beaten up during the gold bear market. Many of these companies made the same mistake I believe companies in the major stock markets are making now. This being when times were good and money was cheap, they took on too much debt and spent the money unwisely. In the gold sector, they used cheap money to take over companies to add to production, and when gold prices dropped, all they had to show for these takeovers was a large amount of debt on their balance sheets, as these properties were not profitable at lower gold prices. In many cases, many of these higher-cost properties have been closed or sold.

American Barrick (ABX NYSE). The poster child for leverage and misallocation of capital in the gold equity arena during the bull market was Barrick Gold. Barrick decided during the bull market cycle to go on a takeover spree and become a massive gold producer. When they did this, they ended up taking over all sorts of properties that were not profitable when gold fell to $1,200 an ounce. This led to massive losses and write-downs and the Barrick stock price falling a great deal. Barrick has made a strategic shift in the last few years of divesting itself of these higher-cost properties and reducing debt.

Since 2015 Barrick has also seen debt fall from $9.6 billion to $5.2 billion. Not many other companies have had a near-40% decline in net debt during this era of cheap money. With Barrick now a much leaner company, I think that makes it a solid conservative investment for investors.

Newmont Mining (NEM NYSE). Like Barrick, Newmont has slowly been paying off debt. Newmont's long-term debt load at the end of fiscal 2015 was $5.8 billion, which it still is today, meaning nine years and basically no net debt has been issued. Newmont took over Goldcorp, another leading large-cap producer. Unlike the takeovers during the gold bull market, this was not an overpayment and was done almost entirely in stock (not debt) and made the company even larger and more diversified. Newmont, like Barrick, is a good, solid conservative play for investors in a potential gold bull market.

Franco-Nevada (FNV NYSE) and Toronto and Royal Gold (RGLD NYSE). These are what are called royalty companies. They are different from regular mining companies in that rather than producing gold themselves, what these companies do is invest in other companies, properties, and mines and then take a percentage of the revenue or profit from that mine. The advantage to this model is that there is more protection to the downside when the market declines. Margins on gold mines are low, and a small drop in prices can wipe out the profits. However, as royalty companies have very little expenses other than the upfront investment, they only see a small decline in royalty revenue rather than profits totally eaten away when gold prices drop.

Royalty companies can diversify themselves. When you invest money for a percent of the revenue, you can invest in properties all over the world. Instead of just having a few producing mines, they can have interests in dozens and dozens of mines. As mentioned earlier, there are all kinds of problems that can happen in mining. An unfriendly government comes and takes the mine from you or taxes a chunk of the profits. You can have a problem at the mine such as a rock fall or an accident stopping production. You could get a glitch, and you hit something that has lower grades and higher cost, cutting into margins and profit.

However, by diversifying and taking a royalty percentage in numerous mines, you protect yourself against these mishaps. It does mean that these companies are not as leveraged on the upside. However, they hold up a lot better during bear markets. In addition, they also can trade at high valuations because the stream of their revenue is so consistent and conservative, the market usually gives them a premium valuation to the rest of the gold sector.

Franco-Nevada and Royal Gold are the two strongest royalty companies trading on the markets. Both have a great track record of success and performed well for decades. The original Franco-Nevada was started by Pierre Lassonde back in the 1980s and was taken over by Newmont mining in the late 1990s.

Pierre then started Franco 2.0 a few years ago, and it has performed wonderfully even in a time of depressed precious metal prices. Since 2011 when most gold stocks have fallen 60%, Franco-Nevada has more than quintupled from just over $25 to over $130! For average investors or investors who don't have a lot of risk tolerance, these well-diversified royalty companies that have steady streams of income are an intelligent way to invest in gold equities.

My advice is when you're looking at a large-cap mining company, look at the large conglomerates or royalty companies. If you really want leverage and possess a higher risk tolerance, I would look more toward the mid-tier and junior companies.

The average investor should have a larger part of their portfolio in the ETFs and large caps and then a smaller amount in the mid-tier and junior companies for leverage. When you're invested in these large caps, you should be looking for capital preservation. The mid-tiers are where you are looking for leverage.

Mid-Tier Gold Equities. These are companies that mainly trade on the major U.S. indexes and usually have one or two or up to a handful of projects either in production or near production. The market caps of these companies usually range from a few hundred million to a couple of billions of dollars. At the bottom of the mining cycle (which is where I believe we are), I like to find mid-tiers that are turnaround plays. As just stated, if you want the stable movement in gold equity, go for the royalty companies or diversified large cap. However, if you want the leverage in the gold price, go for the mid-tier, especially the mid-tier that is beaten up. Ironically, this means finding companies with bad fundamentals, as their prices are super depressed and have the most leverage to the upside if gold turns up in price.

Back in the late 1990s, a company named Eldorado Gold was having all sorts of problems; its mines were not profitable, and it was putting others into production. Some wondered if it would survive with gold prices below $250 an ounce. This caused the price of the stock to drop from $36 Canadian in 1996 to $1 (numbers are post reverse split) in 2001. At the time, I researched the stock and realized that Eldorado would survive because the properties Eldorado operated were about to come into production when gold turned around, which meant that Eldorado could really move to the upside as cash flow would explode as gold prices and production both increased. Long story short, over the next 10 years Eldorado rallied to $80 a share.

Around the same time frame, I recommended a company called Desert Sun Mining at under $1 a share, run by my friend, Stan Bharti, who has a track record of putting companies into production and selling them to majors. Desert Sun had taken over the Jacobina project in Brazil. This was a formerly producing mine that just needed some development of the resource and advancement of the project. Desert Sun increased the resource and put the mine into production. Yamana Gold ended up taking over Desert Sun for over $7 a share and for over $500 million Canadian.

These are the two types of mid-tiers you can look at when you feel you are early in a new bull market cycle for gold equities: one is it's a beaten-up turnaround play, which will rise when the price of gold rises; the other is a newer production play, which has leverage due to the new ounces in the ground and ounces it produces.

Here are a handful of mid-tier companies that are beaten up and I think will turn around as gold rises.

Eldorado Gold (EGO NYSE). Things have come full circle for Eldorado. After soaring to $80 a share, Eldorado has experienced extreme difficulties in the last eight years (since gold entered a bear market). Eldorado took on debt and has had problems with some of its properties. Eldorado's flagship property, the Kisaldag deposit, has experienced higher costs, lower production, and a downgrade in its resources. In addition, they have also had difficulty putting their mine in Greece into production due to government permitting. This has caused Eldorado to fall from $80 a share when adjusted for Eldorado's recent reverse split to as low as $3.50 a share. The positive side is that this decline made Eldorado very cheap. At its lows it traded at a mere one-sixth of book value. Even though Eldorado has rebounded to nearly $15 a share, it still trades at one-fifth of book value!

New Gold (NGD NYSE). This is another turnaround play. New Gold has had many problems with its flagship property in the past few years. The company has not been able to produce as much gold as first anticipated. The cost of production has been much higher than originally thought. The economic nature of the resource has been lower than the company thought as well. This has decimated the price of the stock. New Gold fell to under $1 a share as I write.

Sometimes a company struggling the most has the most leverage when the market turns. For example, let's say company ABC produces gold at $1,600 an ounce with all costs in, and gold is $2,000, so they're making about $400 an ounce. Gold goes to $2,400 an ounce, so they essentially go from making $400 an ounce to $800; maybe the stock price will triple or a bit more if the valuation expands.

With a company such as New Gold, that's losing money, the increase in the price of gold changes the prospects much more dramatically. New Gold is a higher-cost producer that needs higher gold prices to be able to become cash flow positive and profitable. The company could go from losing hundreds of dollars an ounce at $1,800 gold to making hundreds of hundreds an ounce when gold is $2,500. The stock will go up much more than the profitable stock, as it goes from a dire position of losing money to all of the sudden making money. We have already seen the early start of this, as when gold was around $1,800 an ounce in 2022, New Gold was trading at $0.70 a share. As I write in 2024, gold has rallied to over $2,600 an ounce, and New Gold is trading near $3 a share, a nearly 300% gain on a roughly 40% gain in gold prices. In addition, they are about breaking even now, and if gold were to trade to north of $2,700 an ounce, they would become profitable, and I could see the stock really taking off.

When you're buying turnaround companies such as New Gold, it's what John Templeton would call "buying at the point of maximum pessimism." This means that the stock is depressed, trading way under its intrinsic value, and can reverse to the upside.

In the late 1930s, Templeton famously bought a hundred companies that were trading under $1 a share, many of them being railroads. His idea was that with the war underway in Europe, the United States would be producing munitions and supplying machinery such as tanks, planes, and ships to the Allied forces in Europe. Much of this would have to be put on railroads shipped to the East Coast and then again shipped over to the United Kingdom and other European countries.

This would get the railroads and the economy moving again, so you would want to be in these companies. Due to the Great Depression, commercial traffic on railroads had collapsed. Many of these railroad companies were in bankruptcy. What Templeton ended up discovering was that the companies that were profitable and doing relatively well vastly underperformed the weaker companies that were near bankruptcy. The recovery in the economy caused these "weak" companies to emerge from bankruptcy and go from losing money to a position of making money, and they shot up as their fortunes turned for the better. Many of the stronger companies went up 5 or 10 times in value, whereas many of the weaker companies went up 50 or even 100 times in value. Buying these beat-up gold companies now is like Templeton buying those beaten-up railroads back in the 1930s.

During the downturn in gold prices, some companies have been able to keep cash flow positive and earnings profitable. However, some companies like New Gold and Eldorado have had great difficulties and are losing a great deal of money with distressed stock prices. When the market turns, these depressed companies will have more leverage, because they will go from a position of weakness to strength rather than a strong company just going from being strong to even stronger.

Eldorado and New Gold are two higher-beta or more volatile companies that tend to underperform in bear markets but outperform in bull markets. Both stocks crashed nearly 90% during the crash of 2008 when most gold stocks fell roughly 75% or so. In the following three years after the crash, from 2008 to 2011, the average gold stock rallied about 300%, or roughly quadrupling in price. However, Eldorado and New Gold both went up nearly 10 times in price.

Eldorado and New Gold are again in similar situations. Both companies have fallen over 90% from their 2011 highs. The average gold stock is down about 70%. I expect that as gold prices climb and both companies go from a position of weakness to strength, they will again outperform the gold equity sector.

Sandstorm Gold and Metalla Resources (SAND NYSE, AMEX NYSE). Earlier in this chapter, I talked about royalty companies and the benefits they have being well diversified and only having some interest in many mines. However, Royal Gold and Franco-Nevada are well established and have been around a long time. Like in any sector, you want to find the "next big thing," or in the case of royalty, play the next Franco or Royal Gold.

While the royalty model is a great model when working, it's difficult to become a good royalty company. You need skilled management that can find dozens of quality projects to invest money in that will then become cash flow positive for the company. Also, you must find companies or mines that the management are open to taking money for and then in turn pay out a royalty. So it is not as easy as it seems. However, I think it is worth a shot to try to find the next big royalty play, because if you do, they will have a lot more leverage to the upside than the well-established ones.

With Sandstorm and Metalla, you have a mid-tier company and a small-cap company. Sandstorm has a market cap of about $1.6 billion (Franco-Nevada has a market cap of about $25 billion and Royal Gold $8 billion). The company is profitable. Sandstorm did take on a lot of debt to expand their royalty portfolio, but as I outlined, with turnaround plays this makes them more leveraged to the upside as gold climbs. In addition, they have more near-production or near-revenue properties than FNV or RGLD, so as they come online, it should give the company a boost.

Metalla is even smaller with only a $240 million market cap. As of 2024, Metalla has only $4.8 million in revenue (although this is double from 2022); they have more projects that are coming online.

However, again this gives Metalla a ton of upside if gold runs, as these projects and royalties come online in the coming years and gold prices are higher.

While it is always hard to find the next big thing, I think taking small fliers on Sandstorm and Metalla are probably worth it, because if they can become anything nearly as successful as Royal Gold and Franco-Nevada, they should do very well as gold prices climb.

Junior Mining Companies. The third tier of gold and precious metal companies is made up of junior mining companies. Junior mining companies are small micro-cap companies usually possessing market caps under $100 million and sometimes just a few million dollars. If you've ever seen the movie *Gold*, it captures the essence of junior miners. *Gold* is based on mining company Bre-X that became a fraud. However, the concept of a junior miner looking to raise a small amount of capital to drill and develop is how most of these companies are started and operate.

I will quickly go over what you look for in a junior mining company. More than any other sector, junior miners are dependent on management. Because junior mining companies are such small companies with limited capital, they are dependent on the small group of people running the company. They must have the expertise and know-how to find a project, drill it, finance it, develop it, and put it into production, not to mention dealing with permitting, environmental and political issues, and other things that can arise with mining.

I have been in this industry for over 20 years, so I know good management and I know what to look for in these companies. Even though it's a difficult industry with only about 1 in every 1,000 deposits becoming economic, it is worth speculating in juniors because they can have returns in not just hundreds but thousands of percent if you speculate successfully. Buying these companies is very time sensitive. And they are very small, so even a small amount of buying can send them higher. Therefore, I will not be dealing with any individual junior miners in this book.

If you are interested in junior mining companies, I cover them in my newsletter *Profiting From Pessimism* (www.profitingfrompessimism.com). I also participate in private placements and venture capital in the sector. If you are interested in these opportunities, please feel free to contact me and subscribe to this publication, as we often cover them there.

Palisades Holdings Pali (TSX Venture). While I won't recommend individual juniors in this book, I do have an interesting way to play the entire sector, if you are interested. Palisade is run by a friend of mine, Collin Kettell. I met Collin about 10 years ago when he was a 24-year-old kid. What he was doing in terms of investing and building a portfolio of properties blew my mind. I knew he would be one of the big names in mining going forward.

Behold 10 years later, Collin's three major deals—Palisades, New Found Gold, and Nevada King—have a combined market cap of nearly $700 million Canadian.

Whereas most junior mining companies are very small, coming out with market caps in the $10 million–$20 million range or even lower, Collin is a big thinker, putting together huge portfolios of holding. His New Found Gold deal has had some of the highest-grade holes drilled of any company in the past few years, and at one point the company had a market cap north of $1 billion (it's about $450 million as I write in 2024).

Nevada King, Collin's other deal, is one of my favorites, because—full disclosure—I played a part in Collin acquiring its key holding the Atlanta Mine along with my friend Chris Crupi, who unfortunately passed away in 2020 (and whom I dedicate this book to). Along with Atlanta, Nevada King holds many properties in Nevada, which made it the third-largest holder of properties in Nevada (they have spun out these properties into a new company because they were getting no value).

What I like about the Palisades concept is that rather than just owning a basket of juniors, it owns companies that they create, put the properties in, and invest in. And as Collin looks to bring out companies with larger market caps that are liquid, you aren't stuck holding a bunch of micro-cap $5 million companies with no liquidity. Palisades trades at about 40% of its net asset value (NAV), meaning you basically buy their holdings for 40 cents on the dollar!

SILVER

Silver is known as the poor man's gold. If you look at precious metals as a currency, gold would be your dollars and silver would be your cents.

The silver sector is extremely small and is probably most famous or most infamous for the Hunt brothers cornering the market in 1980, which shot the price up from a few dollars an ounce to $50 an ounce! In 2011, silver traded back to that $50 an ounce but has sold off sharply, falling to $15 an ounce in 2019. Silver has more upside to gold in precious metals bull markets and tends to outperform. Silver tends to attract retail investors during bull markets simply due to its price. Smaller retail investors may not be able to afford gold at thousands of dollars an ounce. However, they can afford silver for $20.

Shy of gauging whether silver is a good buy or not when compared to gold is the gold-to-silver ratio. Basically, it's a simple ratio that takes the price of silver and divides it into the price of gold. When it takes more than 50 ounces of silver to buy 1 ounce of gold, you want to buy silver, as silver is cheap compared to gold and outperforms after that. When it only takes 10 to 20 ounces of silver to buy 1 ounce of gold, that's usually when you want to sell, as silver is vastly overvalued and doesn't have an upside relative to the price of gold. Now with gold trading at roughly $2,600 an ounce as I write and silver at only $32 an ounce, this means the ratio is near 83 to 1, which is near historic lows. Whenever the ratio has reached this extreme level, silver has been a great investment.

How to Buy Silver

Like gold, silver has an ETF. The iShares Silver ETF (SLV NYSE) is the silver ETF. This is the easiest way for individual investors to invest in silver. Like gold, you could buy the coins from dealers. In addition, there are silver mining companies, which we will discuss.

The Sprott Physical Gold and Silver Trust (CEF NYSE), which we mentioned earlier, has about a 20% weighting in silver bullion and is another great way to get exposure to silver.

Silver Mining Companies

Silver is a much smaller sector than gold, and there are decisively fewer companies. However, there are still pure silver plays you can invest in.

Wheaton Precious Metals (WPM NYSE). Wheaton Precious Metals is like Royal Gold and Franco-Nevada and is a royalty company. Like those two gold stocks, Wheaton Precious Metals has held up much better than most silver stocks. While most silver equities have fallen 50% or more since 2012, Wheaton is up 40%. It should be noted that Wheaton is not a pure silver royalty play but has much more silver exposure than Royal Gold and Franco as a royalty company.

Pan American Silver (PAAS NYSE). This is one of the largest, most diversified silver companies in the world. Like most of the major gold companies, it has performed very poorly in recent years. Just to show how small the silver industry is, Pan American only has a market cap of $2.2 billion, which would make it a smaller producing company in the gold sector.

This company has survived lower silver prices and has kept its balance sheet in good shape. Pan Am didn't get lured in by cheap money or the hotness of the precious metals sector in the late 2000s and early 2010s.

The company operates mines in Peru, Canada, Bolivia, Argentina, and Chile, making it a very well diversified company on the geographic and political spectrum. I have Pan American as a core holding, if you're interested in investing in silver stocks.

Hecla (HL NYSE). Hecla is one of the oldest silver and precious metals companies in the world. It was founded in 1891. Hecla is primarily a North American producer, with most of its mines located in the United States and Canada. It also operates in Durango, Mexico. Hecla is the anti–Pan American. It took on a great amount of debt and has over $500 million of long-term debt on its balance sheet.

Like I have noted, companies that possess weak balance sheets potentially have the most turnaround potential. Hecla was north of $12 a share at its peak in 2008, so the company has since fallen over 60% in price. The leveraged nature of its balance sheet makes Hecla a large boom-and-bust stock. However, if we see an increase in the precious metals and silver prices over the next few years, Hecla is a type of company that could be leveraged to the upside. This is not a trade for the fainthearted.

What I have given you is one silver company that is one of the most conservative, well-managed companies in the sector, and another silver company that has taken on a lot of debt and leveraged itself and is a turnaround play. If I were an individual investor, I would put more money into Pan American, but Hecla is a very interesting speculative turnaround play.

Endeavour Silver (EXK NYSE). One stock I recently recommended in both the *Financial Intelligence Report* and Profitfrom pessimism.com is Endeavour Silver. This is a great leveraged play on silver. Endeavour is a mid-cap-sized company (roughly $1 billion market cap) that has properties in Chile and the United States.

This is a company I like more because of the technicalities. If you look at a 15-year chart of Endeavour, you will see Endeavour has had a huge history of booms and busts. There have been three occasions—2009 to 2011, 2016, and 2020 to 2021—that Endeavour went from roughly $1–$1.50 a share to $6–$10 a share (in the case of 2011, it went to $12). I saw another opportunity when Endeavour went to $1.50 a share this past spring. If you factor in that the company fell this low with silver around $22 an ounce and the past declines of $1 to $1.50 occurred with silver in the $12 to $14 an ounce range when compared to silver, Endeavour was as cheap as it had ever been. Since then, Endeavour has rallied to $4 a share as I write in mid-2024. I still think it has much more upside (they had a recent problem at their processing mill that caused the stock to drop and has led to another buying opportunity). In addition, if you factor in these other large rallies in Endeavour that have occurred during a near 13-year bear market in silver from 2011 to 2024, imagine what it could do if silver breaks out and enters a new long-term bull market.

PALLADIUM AND PLATINUM

These metals do not operate as the currencies hedges like gold and silver do. Both have usages in catalytic converters for cars and have usages in electronics. What's interesting is that both also have limited supplies in terms of where they are produced.

What's interesting about palladium is most of the production globally comes from two countries: Russia and South Africa.

Therefore, these two countries can influence the price if they decide to cut production, and they have done this in the past. Recently, there has been a large spike in the palladium price due to supply issues.

The fear in the palladium market is that cuts in the usage of gasoline-running cars will kill the long-term demand for it. As you will read in Chapter 8 on clean energy, I do not feel that it's feasible, realistic, or economic that electric cars will totally take over the entire automobile market. Mazda, for example, is going the route of making super highly efficient gas engines rather than going toward electric cars, thus telling us there will always be a market for the combustion engine and palladium.

My palladium stock of choice will be North American Palladium (PALDF) pink sheets. This is the largest producer in North America and is outside the realm of South African and Russian production. They benefit when the Russians squeeze supply, as their stable production in North America allows them to take advantage of the price spikes.

Anglo American (AAL LSE, NGLOY Pink Sheets)

The largest and most diversified platinum producer is Anglo American. This is a mining company that was founded over a hundred years ago. Their properties are all over the world, ranging in resources from coal, to diamonds, to platinum. Anglo American is a very well-managed company; they made over $12 billion in fiscal 2023. Stock pays a near 4% dividend. And they've cut debt from over $16 billion in 2015 to just over $7.5 billion at the end of fiscal 2023. If any downturn in the economy is followed by our prediction of a massive stimulus and "QE for the people," Anglo would be a huge recipient of this stimulus with all the production it has in base metals and platinum.

BASE METALS: COPPER, IRON ORE, AND STEEL

Base metals derive their name from the fact that they are much more abundant than precious metals and are used in every single sector of commerce. Most base metals are used in automobiles, steel and wiring in buildings and bridges, electronics, the list goes on. Base metals, unlike precious metals, are very dependent on performance and demand from the real economy.

One of the biggest drivers of demand for base metals over the past 20 years has been the growth in the emerging world. China, India, Indonesia, Vietnam, and many other emerging markets have increased infrastructure spending and spending modernizing their cities and skylines. By some estimates, nearly 40% to 50% of base metal demand comes from China alone.

Base metals often do not trade with precious metals. Precious metals are seen as a hedge to volatility and a safe haven, so oftentimes gold and silver perform well during bear markets and crises. Contrarily, base metals are usually weak during a crisis or bear market as demand for them wanes.

Copper

A nickname for copper is Doctor Copper. What this means is copper is seen as an indicator for the broader economy. Copper is used in automobiles, apartment buildings, phone lines, bridges, and virtually almost anything you can think of built on a large scale. Therefore, copper tends to be very economically sensitive. During the recession of the early 2000s, copper fell to $0.75 a pound. During the boom of the 2000s, which saw a housing boom in the United States and an infrastructure and spending boom in China, copper rose to nearly $4 a pound. It then crashed to $1 during the financial crisis.

During a huge Chinese stimulus from 2009 to 2011 and U.S. recovery, which featured a $700 billion spending package in the United States, copper rebounded to $4 a pound. As I write, copper is trading just above $4.50 a pound.

In the short term, economic activity will drive copper's price. However, copper has something else interesting going for it in the longer term. In the long term, it looks like a supply shortage is developing in copper. In addition, in the longer term, copper's demand should rise, as it is a key component in electric vehicles. Figure 3.7 is an example of the future demand by electric vehicles for copper. There were an estimated 5 million electric cars sold globally in 2021, and this is expected to increase to more than 70 million per year by 2040.

Therefore, in the next 10 to 20 years we could see a perfect storm for copper with increasing demand and declining production.

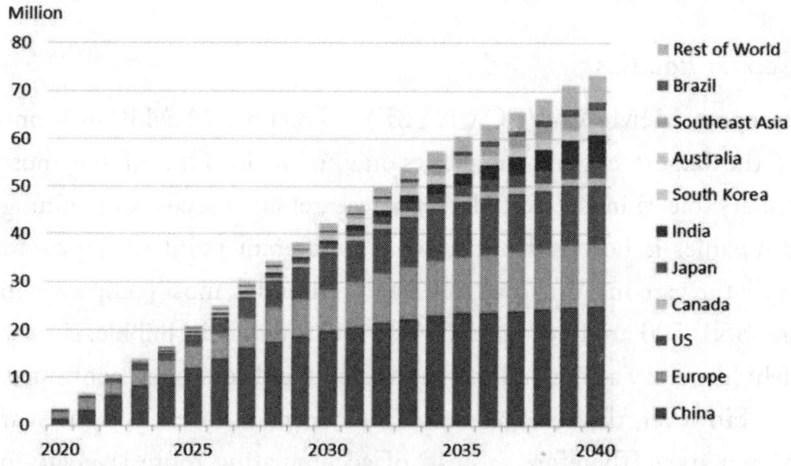

FIGURE 3.7 Global long-term passenger EV sales by market in BNEF's economic transition scenario.

Source: Bloomberg. Courtesy of https://about.bnef.com/blog/electric-vehicle-sales-headed-for-record-year-but-growth-slowdown-puts-climate-targets-at-risk-according-to-bloombergnef-report/

Also, Mining.com notes there will be a huge shortage in copper in the coming years, as it is a prime ingredient needed in electric vehicles:

> According to McKinsey, global electrification is expected to increase annual copper demand to 36.6 million tonnes by 2031, compared to the current demand of roughly 25 million tonnes. However, the consultancy firm forecasts copper supply to be around 30.1 million tonnes, leaving a gap of 6.5 million tonnes by the start of next decade.*

Green uses of copper accounted for 4% of copper consumption in 2020, but this is expected to rise to 17% by 2030, Aditi Rai, an analyst at Goldman Sachs, wrote in a note. He added that a "net-zero emissions" path would mean the world would need an additional 54% of copper by 2030 on top of that forecast.

Copper Equities

Freeport-McMoRan (FCX NYSE). Freeport-McMoRan is one of the largest copper companies in the world. One of the most remarkable things I found when researching metals and mining companies is how you notice what a different point in the credit cycle they are in. As shown in Chapters 1 and 2, most companies in the S&P 500 are in the middle of a credit and debt bubble, issuing debt like crazy as the bull market in credit and stocks has continued.

However, the resource sector has been in a nearly eight-year bear market. Therefore, instead of accumulating more leverage in debt, these companies are reducing debt and leverage. For example, Freeport-McMoRan in 2015 had nearly $20 billion in long-term

---

*Source:https://www.mining.com/the-global-copper-market-is-entering-an-age-of-extremely-large-deficits/.

debt and under $100 million of cash on its balance sheet. The company now has over $4.7 billion in cash and only $9.8 billion in debt. This means if there is a continued bear market in base metals, Freeport should easily be able to withstand it. It also means that when the inevitable turn in the sector comes, it will be an extremely lean company going into the bull market.

Southern Copper SCCO. Another copper company I like is Southern Copper. Unlike Freeport, which is a diversified conglomerate, Southern Copper has most of its operations in Peru. This is a company that has experienced growth in recent years. It has gone from being a smaller mid-tier producer to being a $90 billion company. Southern Copper also pays a hefty dividend of near 3%.

Iron Ore and Steel

Iron ore and steel are two very cyclical industries. In the last 20 years, much of the demand in these industries has come from China. As China has built up the country not just in the two major cities of Shanghai and Beijing, but in all the other second-, third-, and fourth-tier cities, this has led to huge demand for steel, iron ore, and concrete. After a major blow-off in 2011, iron ore and steel stocks have fallen a great deal. Many of the stocks have fallen 90% from their highs. They now represent good value, and if there is "QE for the people," they could have a roaring bull market after the next recession.

Iron Ore and Steel Stocks

Cliffs Natural Resources (CLF NYSE). This is a turnaround play in the iron ore sector. During the bubble and boom, Cliffs made about every mistake a mining company could make. They paid nearly $4 billion for a mine from Consolidated Thompson in

Canada, which was also run by Stan Bharti, then sold it for pennies on the dollar a few years ago. They leveraged their balance sheet with a ton of debt, expanding production right at the top of the market. These errors and lower iron ore prices led to the stock dropping from a high of nearly $100 a share to just $3 a share. Over the last few years, the company has restructured and rebounded to about $16 a share. They have restructured so it has only $22 billion in revenue and $3 billion in debt.

Champion Iron Ore (CIA TSE). Champion Iron Ore is on the other end of the spectrum in terms of management. Where Cliffs is a turnaround play, this is a solidly run company that is growing. They were the company that bought the property from Cliffs for pennies on the dollar and then turned around and put it into production. This property was a struggling property under Cliffs' management, but Champion started mining the property on a small scale, mining the most profitable and low-cost parts of the mine, and now are building up and expanding the mine into full production. This has allowed Cliffs to trade from a penny stock to a near-$6 stock and become a $1 billion Canadian company. The company is a bit overbought right now, but it would be something I would look at on a decline. This company also shows you what happens if you can buy assets cheap. Champion bought their main property very cheap at the bottom of the market and that led to big gains for the stock.

CONCLUSION: DELEVERAGING AND "QE FOR THE PEOPLE"

As you may have noticed, I am really concentrating on the debt loads of resource companies. I am so focused on debt because one of my basic theses is you want to be in sectors that either have little debt or are in cutting-edge growth industries. As resource companies have very little in cutting-edge technology, I want to show you how these companies have become leaner and more efficient in facing the downturn they have faced since 2011. This is opposite to the rest of the stock market, which is seeing companies take on huge amounts of debt over the past 10 years.

Another reason I think that these base metals and miners will be good investments after the next market downturn is my thesis that the next stimulus will be "QE for the people." This means that rather than just having QE going into financial engineering and markets, the stimulus will go into the real economy (e.g., building bridges, roads, infrastructure) and will result in demand for these base metals. This could restart a major bull market in these miners. In addition, QE may be used to fund MMT and universal basic income, which are becoming increasingly common ideologies as populism rises.

I feel gold and precious metal miners will roar as they will again become contrarian investments to the stock market in the economy. As the everything bubble bursts and we see the end of hypernormalization, people will again move into precious metals to hedge themselves as they did in the bear markets of the 1970s, 1980s, and early 2000s.

4

Oil and Gas

One of the practical themes of this book is to encourage others to exercise patience when buying into the sector. As I mentioned earlier, the great investor Kyle Bass theorizes that the average investor's historical time frame and reference is about two years. This means whatever has occurred in the last two years, the average investor projects into the future and thinks that will go on indefinitely.

I saw this phenomenon in action in 2009. In March of 2009, just after the market had bottomed, a friend and I hosted a small investment conference at the Atlantis resort in Nassau, Bahamas. At that conference virtually every attendee was bearish on the equity market. Why? Quite simply put, since the summer of 2007 until March of 2009, the markets had dropped, falling over 50% in price. Because the market had dropped for nearly two years and dropped so ferociously, the attendees bought into the recency bias and thought it would continue to drop. I was the most bullish person at the conference, and I thought we were entering a 2- to 3-year bull market (it's gone up to 10).

Currently, investors believe that stocks will continue to rise because the market has been in a 15-year bull run.

However, these same retail investors are ignoring commodities and believe that they will continue to decline, because they have been in bear markets since 2011. Oil is nearly 50% off its 2008 highs, and many of the oil and gas stocks are down even more.

From Figure 4.1, we can see that commodities compared to stocks are very cheap. Meaning that now is the time you want to own commodities, unlike 2008 when you wanted to sell them. Therefore, I have spent a lot of time on commodities in both Chapters 3 and 4. They are one of the few cheap sectors in the market now, and when they are this cheap, the returns over the next three to five years are usually very strong. The last two times commodities were this cheap compared to the S&P 500 were the early 1970s, which saw a huge boom and bull market in commodities until 1980, and 1999, which saw a near-12-year bull market in commodities into 2011.

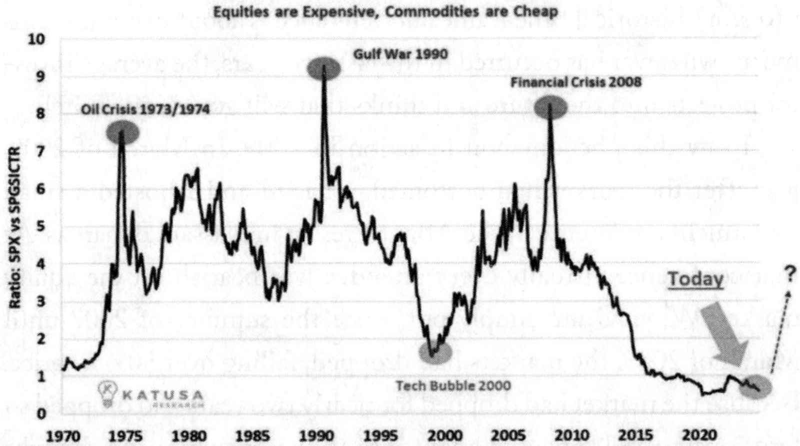

FIGURE 4.1 S&P Commodity Index vs. S&P 500.
Source: www.bloomberg.com. Courtesy: https://x.com/AHzCrypto/status/1834866646055338082

With that being said, I think some commodity equities might need one more leg lower before being great buys. For many of the investments I discuss in this book, I am recommending a dollar-cost averaging approach, as I feel there may be one more leg lower if the S&P 500 and major stock indices see a bear market. My theory is to buy some commodity equities now, then wait for a sell-off to see if things get cheaper, and buy more if they do. If there is a recession in the coming years, there could be a drawdown in commodities, as a decline in markets and the economy could cause a short-term disinflationary cycle.

TABLE 4.1 Performance of asset classes after they drop 60% to 90% in price

Average 3-Year Nominal Returns When Buying a Sector Down Since 1920s:	Average 3-Year Nominal Returns When Buying an Industry Down Since 1920s:	Average 3-Year Nominal Returns When Buying a Country Down Since 1970s:
60% = 57%	60% = 71%	60% = 107%
70% = 87%	70% = 96%	70% = 116%
80% = 172%	80% = 136%	80% = 118%
90% = 240%	90% = 115%	90% = 156%

Source: http://mebfaber.com/2013/06/25/what-happens-when-you-buy-assets-down-80/

As you can see in Table 4.1, when asset classes fall 80% to 90%, they usually climb hundreds of percentage points three years later. In 1997, Asian markets such as South Korea or Taiwan were down 70% from their highs; in 1998, Russia was down over 80%. In 1999 and 2000, gold stocks were down over 70%. In 2001, Argentine stocks; in 2002, U.S. tech stocks. Even during the bull market bubble of the last 10 years, you could have purchased Greek stocks in 2012, Russian stocks in 2014, or Brazilian stocks in 2016 and had one-to-two-year returns superior to the stock market by being patient and waiting for markets to fall 70% to 90%.

Oil and gas was a perfect example of this, as it fell not only 90% in 2020 but over 100% during Covid, as oil traded negative when the global economy came to a standstill for a few months during lockdowns. This caused the XOI, the leading oil and gas index, to crash from over 1,500 to 500; since then, the XOI has more than quadrupled to over 2,000! Yet again, proving another win for buying maximum pessimism.

In past boom cycles in oil and gas, most of the speculative money and exploration money flowed into offshore drilling. However, in the last 15 years, it wasn't offshore drillers that were the recipients of cheap money, but rather the fracking industry. From 2010 to 2014, there was a perfect storm for fracking. Cheap money was looking for higher-yielding returns and high oil and gas prices along with new technologies, which allowed fracking beneath the Permian Basin in the Midwest. This caused a huge boom in many Midwestern states that they had not seen since the 1970s in oil and gas exploration. This has obviously been great for U.S. oil and gas production. U.S. oil production, which had fallen to as low as 5 million barrels a day, has nearly tripled to 13 million barrels a day in early 2024, an all-time high by any country ever!

I believe a lot of this capital has been misallocated. Many of the frackers have taken way too much debt on their balance sheet. They will have problems if the combination of lower oil and gas prices and the deteriorating corporate credit market occurs.

The following excerpt from an excellent article on Oilprice.com shows just how bad the misallocations are. Recently, the Institute for Energy Economics and Financial Analysis, along with the Sightline Institute, wrote in a joint report on the first quarter earnings in 2019 of the shale industry. Commenting on the report, Oilprice.com noted:

> The report studied 29 North American shale companies and found a combined $2.5 billion in negative free cash flow in the first quarter. That was a deterioration from the $2.1 billion in negative cash flow from the fourth quarter of 2018. "This dismal cash flow performance came despite a 16 percent quarter-over-quarter decline in capital expenditures," the report's authors concluded.
>
> The "sector as a whole consistently fails to produce enough cash to satisfy its voracious appetite for capital," the report said. The 29 companies surveyed by IEEFA and Sightline Institute burned through a combined $184 billion more than they generated between 2010.
>
> More than 170 U.S. shale companies have declared bankruptcy since 2015, affecting nearly $100 billion in debt, according to Haynes and Boone. There have been an estimated 8 bankruptcies already this year, with some $3 billion in debt restructured, "haemorrhaging cash every single year."*

One way to gauge when many oil and gas companies may be at the extreme point of pessimism in the next downturn is the junk bond market. Much of the junk bond market is made up of bonds issued in the oil and gas sector and more specifically the fracking sector over the past 15 years. Even with all the losses and negative cash flow, these companies have the market continually fund them. However, there now seems to be a reluctance to issue more debt to these companies. It will be interesting to see how they perform in the next downturn in oil price, especially if it coincides with a freeze-up in the corporate bond markets.

---

* Source: https://oilprice.com/global-energy-alert?utm_medium=inad&utm_source=onsite&utm_campaign=opinad_2.

My prediction is that many of these fracking companies will fail, or many of them will have to do what a lot of the mining companies have done since 2011—this can scale back operations and pay back debt. This means they will have to produce less and concentrate on fewer oil wells that are more profitable. In either case, the companies will take supply off the market, and that will help lead to the final bottom in oil and gas. What you want to do is find the companies that can survive the downturn and profit from the turnaround.

When I think about the fracking boom, it brings me to my favorite stock market movie, which showed how this type of boom and bust happened in the United States once before. When you mention trading movies, most may think of *Trading Places*, *Wall Street*, or *The Big Short*. However, mine is *Splendor in the Grass*, a classic that takes place during the Roaring Twenties. It's most famous for being Warren Beatty's first film; he plays a character named Bud. It's a love story that has the bubble of the 1920s as the backdrop. Bud's father (played by Pat Hingle) is an oil tycoon who has developed a drilling and production company in Kansas (today's fracking boom is also in the Midwest). In one part of the movie, Bud's sister tells their father that "he would drill for oil in their front yard if he thought it was there," to which the father responds he would drill a hole right through the kitchen table if there was oil underneath the house.

The similarity to the 1920s is that there was a cheap money stock market bubble, which filters down to oil and gas as well as other industries. At the end of the movie (spoiler alert if you want to watch it), the 1929 crash occurs. Bud's father commits suicide, and Bud inherits the family property. Due to the crash and Great Depression, Bud turns the house back into a farm and the oil-drilling days are over. This puts the boom-bust into a human context, and it's amazing that no matter how much more advanced we are today in terms of technology, the boom-bust of cheap money just repeats itself. When the cheap money bubble bursts, I expect we could see many similar occurrences in the Midwest with unprofitable fracking wells lying empty just like Bud's father's after the crash.

In addition, what could also lead to lower prices that causes a fracking crash is China slowing. In the last 20 years, 62% of new oil demand has come from China, and China's economy is cooling quickly. Therefore, I think in the short term (the next year or two) this could keep oil prices lower until companies go bankrupt and supply comes offstream.

OIL STOCKS

I'm not going to recommend stocks like Exxon or Chevron. The problem with these integrated multinationals as pure oil and gas plays is that they tend to be more service plays, as on top of production, they resell oil and gas at the consumer level along with food and other goods at their chains of gas stations. These companies have more correlation with the stock market and economy than they do with oil and gas prices.

When purchasing oil and gas companies, my belief is that you want to buy companies that possess leverage to the price of the underlying commodity. The companies that are most leveraged by the price are the drilling service companies such as Schlumberger and Halliburton. The reason that drilling service companies are so volatile is because of the leveraged nature of the oil drilling service business.

Service companies help oil companies with expert services such as stimulation and sand control services, as well as cementing services, such as bonding the well, well casing, and casing equipment. They also provide completion tools that offer downhole solutions and services, including well completion products and services, intelligent well completions, liner hanger and sand control systems, and service tools; production solutions comprising coiled tubing, hydraulic workover units, and downhole tools; pipeline and process services such as precommissioning, commissioning, maintenance, and decommissioning, plus much more. Most oil companies tend to drill and look for more production and use service companies when prices are high and it's economical to look for new oil.

When there's a downturn in the oil price and margins are squeezed, oil companies usually cut exploration budgets first, as it's not economical to explore for new oil and gas at low prices; they are the easiest thing to cut.

For example, Schlumberger over the last 20 years has traded between $20 and $120 a share this year and plunged to nearly $20—a 25-year low! Halliburton traded as low as $5 in 2002, with its highest $70 in 2014 in the last 20 years and trading as low as $7, nearly 90% off its high.

It should be noted that these are two of the largest, most diversified companies in the drilling service sector. Both survived the bust of the 1980s that saw oil fall to below $10 a barrel, the sub-$20 prices of the late 1990s, and the 2008 financial crisis. Therefore, I would expect these to be excellent leveraged plays once oil does bottom and turn around. If there is a global recession and downturn, oil should continue to fall in price and the oil drilling stocks may fall further and become great buys. A major factor in oil prices weakening at the moment is that China's economy is struggling and China has represented nearly 65% of new oil demand for oil in the last 20 years.

In 2008 Halliburton fell from north of $50 a share to $16, then rallied back to over $70 by 2014. Schlumberger fell from over $100 a share to $33 during the financial crisis, then rallied back to $117 by 2014. Therefore, if these companies have panic lows during a crisis or recession, they should be followed by strong reflexive rallies.

Canadian Oil Sands Companies

Another aspect of oil and gas that benefited from the cheap money boom was the oil sands in Canada. This boom began before fracking back in the early 2000s. Drilling the oil sands in Canada is a very difficult process and an expensive form of oil exploration. It basically separates tar from the oil underneath the earth's surface. However, the discoveries tend to be large and have long shelf lives. Therefore, when you discover oil in the oil sands in Alberta, the projects tend to have years if not decades of production.

The oil that is found in the tar sands, because it's heavier, tends to sell at a lower price. In addition, Canada has had an unfriendly government toward the oil sands for the last four years, and this has also hurt the oil sector. Alberta, where the oil sector is located, is landlocked and the easiest route of transportation for the oil is via pipeline. However, there has been no definite plan for a pipeline either to the West Coast with oil to be shipped to China or through the plains into the United States or to eastern Canada. A lot of the oil that is produced is just sitting there stuck in Alberta and must be shipped via rail or truck. This also depresses the price, as companies become even more willing to sell it at a lower price just to move it out. But if they could just sell after production, they could sell at closer to market price, as it would not just be sitting in inventory.

Oil Sands Plays: Suncor Energy (SU NYSE) and Athabasca (ATH Toronto)

The decline in oil prices and these logistical and political problems have created real value in the sector. The leading company in the oil sands is Suncor (SU NYSE). Suncor was a growth company in the 2000s as production in the oil sands exploded. Suncor is now a very large, stable oil producer. It trades at a low valuation and yields nearly 4%.

A favorite play in the oil sands is Athabasca (ATH) Toronto, which has turned around. This is a smaller producer which IPO'd near the top of the resource market in 2011. The stock fell from this $18 price to under $0.10 a share in 2020! Since then, Athabasca has rallied back to over $5 a share as oil prices recovered. However, the stock is still cheap, trading at a single-digit P/E.

A catalyst for these Canadian companies is a potential turnaround in the political environment in Canada. As noted, the current government of Canada is very unfriendly to the oil sands and oil sand companies, implementing all sorts of carbon taxes and restrictions on pipelines. In the 2025 Canadian election, the much more energy friendly Conservative Party is well ahead in the polls and should win in a landslide, and there should be a big push toward a pipeline being built and it will be much easier for these companies to operate and increase production.

AGRICULTURAL COMMODITIES

Trading commodities is a lot different than trading stocks. While there are some fundamental factors, seasonal supply, and demand factors in agricultural commodities, much of the trades are based on technical analysis.

One factor that makes many of these commodities much different than equities is they are not in a super long-term uptrend like equities. The Dow Jones Industrial Average was 1,400 in 1983, and it is over 39,000 as I write in 2024. However, soybeans, which traded at $9 in 1983, trade at $11! Adjusted for inflation, that is a much lower level than in 1983. Despite this long-term underperformance, over those 40-plus years due to the volatility and leverage of commodities, you can use the commodities markets for opportunities that a trader could take advantage of.

Traders in agricultural commodities are not looking for long-term gains but rather trades. They look for big moves where they can leverage these moves in the futures market. I only recommend trading in the futures market if you are an expert trader. However, there are ways retail traders can trade these markets.

As an example, there was an interesting situation that occurred in agricultural commodities, which brought a great opportunity. In early 2019 there was near-record flooding in the Midwest in the United States. This really hindered the planting of crops and the quality of the crops produced in 2019. As a result, Deere, the maker of John Deere tractors, reported a dismal quarter in early 2019 where the stock gapped down due to lack of demand. The reason for this lack of demand for tractors had nothing to do with the economy and was just weather related. With the floods making farmland unfarmable, there was less demand for tractors until this land could recover from these storms. After 2019 Deere shot up from $125 a share to almost $400 in 2023, more than tripling in price.

Most agricultural commodities have been in long bear markets since 2011. In 2011 there was a large amount of flooding like today, which helped contribute to those price spikes. After some of these huge price increases, the natural reaction was farmers around the world began planting more and more of the commodities that spiked, as they could sell their product for more. This caused a rebound in supply, and prices of these commodities have trended lower since.

Wheat spiked to $9 a bushel in 2012, then fell to as low as $3 in 2019; corn rose to $8 a bushel, then fell to just over $3; and soybeans prices fell from $17 in 2012 to $6 in 2019. All these commodities shot up in price in the years that followed.

The commodity markets trade a lot on technical charting and supply issues that can trigger higher prices, and these higher prices could then trigger technical traders to buy. Many traders in the agricultural commodities trade solely on charts. Therefore, if these commodities begin to break key resistance levels, this may trigger technical buying and send prices even higher. If you look at the trading action in these commodities, what occurs historically is that they trade in a base for a long period of time and have specific resistance levels. When they break these resistance levels, they usually have big moves out of the base.

For example, wheat in 2010 had resistance in the $6 area. When it broke, it quickly climbed to $8.50 for a gain of 40% after it broke out. Corn in 2010 had resistance at $4.50; when it broke that level, it climbed to $8 in just a few months. Therefore, a trading strategy for agricultural commodities is to spot a certain resistance level and then buy when they break resistance for a year.

When you are trading like this, you are not worried about getting the entire trade. If you can get a quick 60%, 70%, or 80% gain in just a few months, that is what you're looking for. This is another advantage of trading commodities: most stocks, other than maybe when they're coming out of a severe decline after being in a bear market, do not experience 50% to 100% returns in just a few months. However, this is quite common in agricultural commodities.

A classic trade in commodities that recently happened was in cocoa. Cocoa had been in a nearly 15-year base trading in a range of $3.50 on the upside and $2 on the downside. In early 2024, cocoa broke this base and soared to $11! Whoever bought the breakout in cocoa at $3.50 and "rode the cocoa comet" in the futures market would have made a fortune.

The great thing for retail traders is all these commodities have ETFs. Before recently, the only way to trade agricultural commodities was through the futures market (think the movie *Trading Places* with Dan Aykroyd and Eddie Murphy), which required a great deal of leverage. The Teucrium corn ETF trades under the ticker CORN NYSE and the Teucrium wheat ETF under the ticker WEAT NYSE. The good news is that both commodities are now cheap again. They spiked during the Russian invasion of Ukraine in 2022 but have since declined, as the supply fears did not take hold. At the levels they are trading at as I go to print, wheat and corn are probably worth small positions in. And the great thing about these ETFs is you do not have to time the market like futures trading does.

Do You Like Sugar in Your Coffee?

Two examples of commodities that were depressed and then soared were coffee and sugar. A few years ago, both were trading at historical levels where they usually have large rallies in price and they did so.

Coffee became extremely depressed in 2019, hitting $0.90, a near-14-years low! Then from 2019 to 2022, coffee rallied nearly three times in price, climbing to $2.60 in 2022. The way you can play coffee is with the IPath Series B Bloomberg Coffee ETF, which trades under the ticker JO NYSE.

Sugar is also beaten up. Sugar, which hit a high of $0.30 a pound in 2011, fell to $0.09 a pound in 2020, which was a near-13-years low. After this, sugar also nearly tripled in price to $0.26 in 2023. If it can break that like coffee, it should have another run higher. The iPath Bloomberg Sugar ETF trades under the SCGFF pink sheets.

It should be noted that many commodities (wheat, corn, etc.) that I have noted are extremely beaten up. Most of them have fallen 50% to 70% from their 2011 highs and are basing. I figure they will break out of these bases when the Federal Reserve reverses course and cuts interest rates, then again does some form of QE. When the Federal Reserve loosened policy in 2008 and 2009, and 2001 and 2002, agricultural commodities vastly benefited from this.

CONCLUSION

I still think in the long run we are in an inflationary cycle. As Milton Friedman once said, inflation is and always has been a monetary phenomenon. With the deficit over $2 trillion for fiscal 2024 and the national debt over $36 trillion, I think even with spending cuts, money printing will have to be used to inflate away the debt, as it is now too large to cut away with austerity.

Commodities are also at the cheapest level they have ever been compared to equities. When I wrote my first book, *Stock Market Panic!*, in 1998 at the tender age of 20, my basic thesis was that commodities were cheap and the market was expensive. Here we are 26 years later, and I have longer, grayer hair and a slightly larger waist size, and it looks like again equities are expensive and commodities are cheap.

With oil experiencing excessive supply and the slowing of the global economy, I could see a bust needed to reduce supply, but at that point many oil stocks will become great buys.

Finally, while most commodities are not to be bought and held long term, I have given techniques here to trade them when they have their spike moves.

5

India, Emerging Markets, and the Future of Real Estate

One of the most unexpected aspects of this most recent 15-year equity bull market from 2009 to 2024 in American stocks has been the underperformance of emerging markets. After the Asian crash in the crisis of 1997 and 1998, Asian markets outperformed developed markets up until 2008.

What makes this underperformance even more bizarre is most of the organic or "real" growth in the world has come from Asia and emerging markets. In the developed world, we have been dependent on asset bubbles, stumbling from bubble to bubble to create growth. In the 1990s there was the dot-com bubble, in the 2000s the housing bubble, and in the 2010s the everything bubble. In the developed world, we have been dependent on creating wealth through financial instruments that create a trickle-down effect for growth. However, in most emerging economies they have organic growth as they grow from third-world countries to richer countries.

Think of the transformation that occurs when a country experiences growth in their emerging markets in the manner China, India, or Indonesia has. In the developed world, we take for granted many infrastructure luxuries such as highways and developed metropolitan areas. These are things that all must be built in many developing countries, and the profits used to fund this expansion generally come from emerging markets. Shantytowns and favelas must be converted into high-rise apartments. Dirt roads must be paved. The middle class who works and keep the gears turning in these emerging markets will eventually wish to move out of small apartments and purchase houses or land. People will start to use things like air-conditioning or purchase their first car. Basic demand for goods and services like these that we have become accustomed to in the West translate into huge growth in the emerging markets.

Since the financial crisis and even before the Covid-19 pandemic of 2020, India and China continued to grow between 5% and 7% a year (even with China slowing as of late). Many other emerging markets that people ignore, like Indonesia, the Philippines, and Malaysia, are growing at a rapid rate. However, their markets have lagged developed markets—especially the American market during this bull market. Currently, the price-to-sales evaluation of the emerging world is lower than it is in developed markets. This is incredible when you consider the rapid pace of growth in emerging markets in said developing countries when compared to developed markets.

Figure 5.1 shows the U.S. stock market capitalization as a percentage of the global stock market capitalization. This peaked during the 2000 dot-com bubble at roughly 50%. This means that U.S. stocks were half the value of the total world stock market. It fell to 30% during the 2000s as the U.S. market recovered from the dot-com bust. The U.S. market has again rallied to nearly 50% of the total world market cap even though the U.S. is roughly 20% of the global GDP. This tells us that the rest of the world and especially emerging markets are very cheap when compared to the U.S. at the moment.

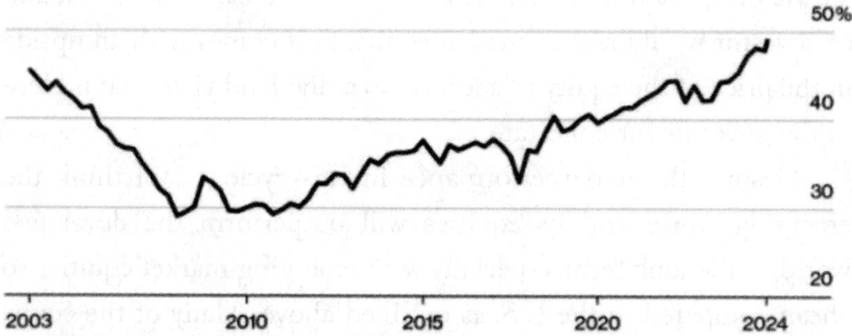

FIGURE 5.1 U.S. percentage of global market cap.
Source: Bloomberg. Courtesy of https://x.com/Barchart/status/1861221410405769281/photo/1

So the question arises: Why did emerging markets perform so poorly during this recovery?

I think the answer to this question goes back to the current bubble we are experiencing, which has been based on cheap interest rates and financial engineering. Many of the emerging markets still have significant interest rates. For example, in 2019 the 10-year bond in India yielded nearly 7%, in Brazil it yielded nearly 8%, and in Sri Lanka it was near 10%, a trend in countries throughout southeast Asia. These countries did not have access to the ultra-cheap money, used to inflate asset prices through borrowing used to fund stock buybacks. In addition, as corporations in the emerging world are still growing organically, they are not obsessed with stock buybacks and financial engineering. A lot of the demand for equities in our market has come from corporations buying their own stock in the United States in the form of buybacks, whereas this buying does not exist in the emerging world.

In addition, higher interest rates can depress stock valuations. Those higher rates in the emerging world's markets depress stock valuation. The reason being that investors may want to own an

Indian bond that yields 7% or 8% rather than an Indian equity. Whereas in North America and Europe when government bonds are yielding 0% to 3%, there is no incentive to own that bond, and an investor would rather own an equity, as it comes with an upside in the price of the equity in addition to a dividend yield that is close to the government bond rate.

Despite the underperformance in this cycle, I still think the emerging world and its equities will outperform the developed world in the long term, especially with emerging market equities so cheap compared to the U.S. as outlined above. Many of the countries in Asia, especially India, have strong demographics and long-term growth potential.

WILL A MILKSHAKE SHAKE OUT AND CRASH EMERGING MARKETS BEFORE THEIR NEXT BOOM?

As I am going to press, many of the major emerging market currencies (e.g., the Indian rupee, Brazilian real, Russian ruble) are tanking as money rushes into the U.S. equities and the U.S. dollar in light of the post-Trump victory rally. A theory by Brent Johnson of Santiago, called the Dollar Milkshake Theory, suggests that the strong U.S. economy and monetary policy will attract capital from other countries, similar to how a milkshake will attract customers at a diner. Here are some important implications inside financial markets. There will be increased demand for the U.S. dollar. With the pro-growth policies of Trump, people are rushing into U.S. assets and selling out of emerging markets as I write in the fall of 2024. The market is expecting tax cuts, smaller government, deregulation, and the movement of investing into the states, as tariffs will force some companies to produce things inside the United States. The idea is this will continue to cause the U.S. dollar to move higher and cause a huge blow-off and boom and bubble in U.S. assets.

There are dangers to this. A devaluation of the Thai baht (a tiny currency) in 1997 led to the Asian crisis of 1997–1998, which took global markets and a large hedge fund (Long-Term Capital Management [LTCM]) down with it, not to mention that it led to a Russian default in 1998.

The BRICS—Brazil, Russia, India, China, and South Africa—are now seeing massive currency devaluations. If this blows up, it could lead to the 1998-style meltdown and much worse, as these economies are much bigger than Thailand and Taiwan and the Asian countries that blew up in 1998.

Another example of the Milkshake Theory and how money has flowed into the United States over the past decade is the outperformance of U.S. equities against European equities, as shown in Figure 5.2. This figure shows that the United States is now outperforming Europe by over 3.5 standard deviations. The figure also shows how cheap European equities are compared to U.S. equities, or it could also be said how expensive U.S. equities are compared to European equities.

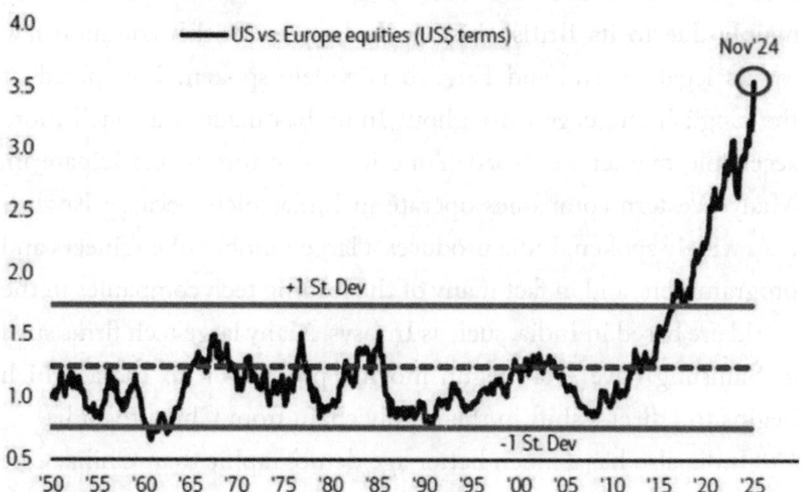

FIGURE 5.2 U.S. stocks very "exceptional" relative to European equities. Source: BofA Global Research. Courtesy of https://x.com/porterstansb/status/1863619200037634296

I also believe there are flaws in the milkshake argument: when you are the reserve currency of the world, you get a flight to safety when crashes and crises happen. In 2000–2001, 2008, and 2010 where there were big market downturns and crises, the U.S. dollar rallied. So a lot of the dollar's rally can be investors moving into the safety of the reserve currency. The British pound saw this happen in the early 1930s when at the depth of the Great Depression the pound hit a record 5 to 1 to the U.S. dollar as it went up in a time of crises in the economy and liquidity.

Still, if a strong "milkshake dollar rally" makes emerging markets cheap, it could bring a great buying opportunity to already cheap markets.

INDIA

India seems to have the potential to be the ultimate long-term investment. India is an interesting investment to look at. It has hundreds of dialects and numerous religions; it is a complex country mainly due to its British history. India uses British common law for its legal system, and English is widely spoken. The spread of the English language throughout India has made it a much more accessible market for North American investors to participate in. Many Western companies operate in India solely because English is so widely spoken. India produces a large number of engineers and programmers, and in fact many of the leading tech companies in the world are based in India, such as Infosys. Many large tech firms such as Samsung have even begun moving production to India, which begins to reflect a shift in the supply chain from China to India.

India also has a much better age demographic than China. One of the major problems China will face in the future is that China is going to get old before it becomes rich. Due to China's one-child policy, the generational age gap has become disproportional, and in a few decades, their population growth will likely begin to decline. Incredibly, the average age of a person in China will be higher than the average age of a person in the United States in 15 years! In 15 years, the average age of a person in India will be roughly 15 years lower than the average age of a person in the United States. If the projections hold true, in the year 2040 a person of average age in India will be in their peak earning years. This tells us in the next 20 to 30 years India should go through a transformation much like China did in the 1980s, 1990s, and 2000s and see rapid growth, meaning that India's markets could become a lucrative investment.

Although its population demographic seems promising, India still has many problems of its own. The infrastructure is archaic when it comes to transportation and housing. It will be very susceptible to Covid spread as its population is so condensed. Furthermore, it is very difficult for the government to manage a democracy of over 1 billion people with varying religious and ideological beliefs. It is very difficult to have a uniform policy across the region, as certain provinces will have different views toward development than other provinces due to their religious or political views. In a way this also works to India's advantage. Rather than growing in a centrally controlled economy like China's, India is growing in a chaotic and unorganized way almost like the United States during its Industrial Revolution. The United States was not a centrally planned economy in the nineteenth century and saw rapid chaotic growth, so India may fall into a very similar cycle.

The Indian stock market is interesting because it's so cyclical, experiencing huge booms and busts. The Sensex stock exchange, the major index in India, has risen from over 2,500 to nearly 80,000 since the early 2000s to the present. This is a gain of nearly 1,600%. However, during this time, the Indian currency has devalued, so in U.S. dollar terms, the returns are not quite impressive. India's history over the last 20 years has been large bull markets followed by severe bear markets when there is a global bear market. These bear markets bring great investment opportunities. For example, the Bombay Stock Exchange rose from 2,500 to over 20,000 from 2001 to 2007 and then fell to 7,500 in 2008. Then after that low of 7,500, it rose to nearly 80,000. So again, this is another patient trade. You do not want to chase the Indian market; rather buy it after one of these large drawdowns. It should be noted that recently the rupee has been falling, so in U.S. dollar terms the Indian market has been falling in 2024.

I would patiently wait and have a few Indian stocks on your shopping list to look at for a potential Indian drawdown. Someone in the future will undoubtedly make a fortune from being able to analyze and pick out Indian small- and mid-cap companies. There are literally hundreds of these companies trading on the Bombay exchange, yielding gigantic dividends. However, for this book and the average investor, I will focus on a few of the key Indian large-cap companies that seem to be promising for the longer term.

The India Fund (IFN NYSE)

This is the simplest and easiest way to buy India. The India Fund is an ETF that owns large-cap stocks in India. When you adjust the India Fund for dividends, you would see that the India Fund has outperformed the S&P 500 going back 20 years! It pays a near-10% dividend. As noted previously, every 10 to 15 years India sees a 50% to 60% drawdown or more. My plan for the India Fund is to average down every 15% to 20% it drops. It has dropped about 20% in early 2024 as I write, so I bought my first tranche.

Tata Motors (TATAMOTORS Sensex)

Tata Motors is one of my favorite stocks. When you look at automobile companies around the world, they usually have a foothold in their own country. In Japan most people buy Japanese vehicles. In Germany most people buy German cars. When you travel to Italy, you see a slew of Alfa Romeo and Fiats on the road. Even in the United States where the foreign car market is huge, the two largest sellers are still Ford and GM. Where China does not really have a domestic automaker, India does. Tata Motors has its own line of domestic vehicles in addition to owning and operating Land Rover and Jaguar. They will be spinning off Jaguar into a separately operated car unit, so by investing in Tata you will have interest in both companies once this spin-off is complete!

In 2009 during the financial crisis, I noted in my newsletter that I purchased Tata Motors at $3.50. Over the next five years, the company soared to as high as $50. I slowly sold on the way up, but it was a classic case of maximum pessimism. At the time I knew that Tata Motors wouldn't go under, and the worst-case scenario would be the Indian government would give them a bailout loan. Owning the higher-end Land Rover and Jaguar brands helped leverage Tata to the global recovery.

Tata gave investors a second chance to buy in 2020; it had slowly moved down from that $50 high for years, then smashed down during the Covid crash to $5 a share. Tata has since delisted from the NYSE and trades only in India, but if you were to use its current price in rupee terms converted to U.S. dollars, Tata is trading at the equivalent of $100 a share. (Tata delisting from NYSE is interesting, as it shows you that companies do not have to list in the United States anymore to survive.) Obviously, at these levels I cannot recommend it. But if it busts again, I would be all in on Tata. Obviously, you would need to use a trading platform like Interactive Brokers, and so on, that can trade foreign stocks. Having access to Indian stocks is probably not a bad idea, as it will be a huge growth market.

Infosys (INFY NASDAQ)

This is one of the largest outsourcing companies in the world. Infosys is known for its phone rooms and outsourcing for large tech companies and customer support. However, the company has really expanded and broadened its portfolio. It's now involved in consulting for infrastructure, financial services, and other industries. Its parlay into financial services should be especially profitable in the future, because as India develops, there will be more demand for loans in terms of automobile, credit, and housing loans. The fees from financial services will explode, and thus the expansion of Infosys into this sector will end up being quite profitable.

However, as keeping in tune with a lot of the investments in this book, I believe you need to have patience with Infosys. India is a boom-bust market and has seen a big boom in asset markets in recent years. Infosys's stock has been on quite a run. After bottoming at near $1 a share right after the dot-com bust, Infosys is now trading at nearly $19 a share. During the dot-com bust, Infosys fell from $6 to $1 a share and during the financial crisis from $6 to $2.50 a share. Therefore, in the last two bear markets, Infosys fell roughly 80% and 60%. I would not be chasing Infosys at these levels, but if it experiences another 60% to 80% drawdown in a bear market, I think at those levels it would represent a great long-term buy. In addition, Infosys pays over a 2% dividend, making it unique for tech companies, as most tech companies pay little to no dividends.

CHINA

I am not as nearly bullish on China as I am India. The main reason for this is due to its centrally planned economy. Many see this planning in a positive light, as China has been able to continually enact government-run stimulus to grow its economy. However, I think this intervention has led to huge dislocations, malinvestments, and a credit bubble in China.

Since 2008, every time the Chinese economy has experienced a slowdown, the government has enacted a large stimulus. They did this from 2009 to 2010 and then again from 2015 to 2016 after the economy was slowing. Every time they do this, they put off a bust, but the dislocations and bubbles get bigger and bigger, and the stimulus needed to grow the economy becomes larger as well.

The need for larger and larger stimulus programs is occurring at a time when China's current account surplus is shrinking. (The current account records a nation's transactions with the rest of the world—specifically its net trade in goods and services, its net earnings on cross-border investments, and its net transfer payments—over a defined period, such as a year or a quarter. The large current account surplus China ran for years helped it fund these stimulus programs. One reason that Japan has not had a major crisis in the past 20 years despite the huge government debt load is because Japan typically runs a current account surplus helping to fund its deficits. China's shrinking current account means that it is in danger of not being able to repeatedly bail out its economy with stimulus payments, which could lead to a major financial meltdown.

With Trump reelected, there could be increased tariffs. For example, China, not the United States, is now the largest producer of electric vehicles (EVs) in the world, and Trump will put heavy tariffs on Chinese EVs to protect Tesla and other U.S. auto manufacturers. This means in terms of tariffs and the trade war, China is much more dependent on demand from the United States than the United States is from China. Most Chinese exports are finished goods. Electronics, pharmaceutical drugs, mechanical devices—these are the types of goods that China commonly exports to the United States; whereas raw materials are mostly exported to China. After covering up the initial outbreak of Covid, much of the world has lost trust in China, and I see supply chains moving. For example, pharmaceuticals will almost surely move the production of drugs back to the United States after seeing the failure of producing them in China. Apple, as another example, has moved a huge amount of iPhone production to India from China in recent years.

There will also be demand globally for agriculture, whereas the demand for Chinese goods is very specific to and dependent on the United States. Therefore, you could argue it will be much easier for the U.S. exporters to find markets for these goods.

The U.S. tariffs on China hurt U.S. multinationals more than the United States itself. For example, Apple, Google, or any company whose cell phones or computers are manufactured in China has a set amount of demand they expect from the United States. It's not that Apple cannot make money producing an iPhone in the United States; this is a fallacy promoted by the company and those in the tech community. The problem for Apple is that Apple would not be able to make the large margins it does currently without the use of cheap labor and the cheap cost of production in China. However, the ethicality and working conditions of these factories have begun to come into question internationally.

In addition, doing business with China has all sorts of security concerns that you do not have when trading and doing business with other countries. We are seeing this with the concerns over Huawei. Huawei has been one of the leaders in 5G technology. The company has also been known for years for stealing other technologies and repackaging them into their own. This could prompt countries to use providers other than Huawei for 5G. Many electronic devices such as smartphones and even police drones are manufactured by Huawei, but consumers have begun to expect many of these products to have built-in "backdoors" or ways to spy on American civilians. This notion of a lack of privacy and security may lead to a shift in where we purchase these goods.

China's 2025 strategy is to become self-sufficient in sectors and goods. We must remember China still does not have much of a domestic aerospace, instead on Airbus and Boeing in aerospace and relying greatly on German, American, and Japanese automakers for gas-powered cars. China 2025 will aim to develop domestic industries to compete with these foreign industries. We are seeing this in industries such as EVs where China is now the largest producer of EVs in the world.

I believe the real issue in China will be the earlier mentioned credit bubbles. There is potential for China to end up like Japan. In the 1980s, Japan had a huge export-oriented economy that was based on an asset bubble. When the Japanese bubble burst, the government did not let the economy cleanse itself. It propped up zombie companies and zombie banks after the bust. On top of that, Japan kept doing fiscal stimulus over and over to prop up its economy. China looks like it is in the same boat. As most of the banks and financial institutions in China are linked to the central government, they will probably be propped up during an economic crisis.

It cannot be understated just how much larger the Chinese real estate and banking bubble is than the American bubble. By most estimates, the U.S. banking system at the peak of the housing bubble was about $17 trillion, and there was another $5 trillion to $6 trillion of assets in Freddie Mae and Fannie Mac, totaling to about $22 trillion to $23 trillion. At that time the U.S. economy was roughly $15 trillion in size, meaning the banking system was about 150% of GDP. After said crash, it took about a $800 billion bailout to recapitalize the banking system.

The Chinese economy is roughly $18.5 trillion in size, and that's if we can fully trust their reported numbers. Chinese financial statements are difficult to analyze unless one is fluent in Chinese, so it is difficult to know just how large the banking system is there. Conservative estimates have the banking system being nearly $60 trillion in size! This means their banking system is double the size that the Americans were right before the financial crisis, and that is with a smaller economy. This goes to show just how devastating a banking crisis could be in China, if one occurs.

In an emerging market with 1.4 billion people, there will be economic opportunities. However, I think that due to the trade concerns, poor age demographics, and its current bubble-like economy, which is stimulus dependent on the central government, China's negatives outweigh the positives.

The Chinese equity market is not open to foreign investors. Foreign investors can buy stocks in countries like Japan, Singapore, Thailand, South Korea, and India, but they cannot directly purchase Class A Chinese shares on the Chinese market. It's a one-way street, with China listing over $1 trillion of securities in the United States but U.S. companies unable to list in China, and this is extremely problematic.

If China has a large bust, there will be maximum pessimism trade opportunities. The Hong Kong Hang Seng Index, which is a proxy market for China and one that foreigners can buy, hit a 27-year low in January of 2024. So while I am not hugely bullish on China's, when markets become that cheap, they are worth looking at. I think that if these opportunities arise in that manner, an investor might want to take advantage by purchasing a U.S.-based company that has an interest in China. One such company would be Skyworks (SWKS NASDAQ), a microchip company that has most of its production in China. Casino stocks such as Las Vegas Sands (LVS NYSE) is another prime example, which now has large operations in Macau that account for more of its revenue than its Las Vegas operations.

TURKEY, BRAZIL, AND ARGENTINA—THE BOOM-AND-BUST ECONOMIES

Whereas India is our long-term play on global growth and emerging markets, Argentina, Brazil, and Turkey are our maximum pessimism trades (especially Argentina). During the 1997 to 1998 Asian financial crisis, there were a ton of investment opportunities among these countries. One notable transaction was a trade by Sir John Templeton when he purchased South Korean stocks. They melted down nearly 70% from top to bottom, as these markets crashed that year. After the crash, South Korea reformed and modernized its economy, aided by the IMF bailout. These reforms and the ensuing recovery allowed the South Korean market to soar over 100% into the year 2000. From 1997 to 2007, South Korea vastly outperformed the U.S. stock market.

In 1998 Russia had a complete and utter economic meltdown. They defaulted on their debt, and their currency collapsed. Russia went into hyperinflation, and their market fell nearly 95% in U.S. dollar terms! The Russian market subsequently was one of the top performing markets in the world. The Russian Trading System Index traded from a low of just under 50 in 1998 to over 2,400 in 2008, an unheard-of return of over 5,000%! Imagine getting in on that investment prior to the collapse.

The following are three emerging markets that I think can potentially bust, then boom and present similar opportunities to what happened in South Korea in 1997 and Russia in 1998, leading to a quite lucrative opportunity if played correctly.

Turkey

Virtually all emerging market booms and busts follow the same script. For whatever reason, there is a period of boom and expansion. These booms tend to see a lot of foreign money coming in. These countries experiencing the boom have cheap credit, and it's also run on a current-account deficit. The funds coming into the country help finance this deficit. The boom turns to bust, and the funds rapidly exit the country. As emerging markets are not as developed or as liquid as developed markets, when this money leaves, it's like an elephant going through a peephole. There is a massive decline in stock markets and the currency. Interest rates are then hiked to ridiculous levels to bring down inflation and to try to keep money in the country and support the currency.

What helped drive the bubble and boom in Turkey was a mix of cheap money and populism. When interest rates in the developed world were cut to near zero, many Turkish companies took advantage of this by issuing debt in U.S. dollars. Turkish corporate debt issued in U.S. dollars yielded more than U.S. treasuries or European bonds. This caused an inflow of money into the debt of Turkish companies, as there was a reach for yield.

In addition, President Recep Tayyip Erdoğan wanted to show that Turkey was strong and going through an economic expansion. He promoted policies that led to a huge real estate buildup and boom around the country. Istanbul, which previously had a unique middle-aged-looking skyline, is now littered with skyscrapers. Turkish companies owe approximately $146 billion in foreign debt. When you factor in that the Turkish currency has fallen over 70% against the U.S. dollar, this will make this debt increasingly difficult to service.

A potential crisis in Turkey could bring a great buying opportunity. There's an old Chinese saying, "The crisis equals opportunity." We have previously stated that John Templeton used to say you want to buy at the point of maximum pessimism. George Soros has said that markets are reflexive and overshot to one side, which then presents a great opportunity. Another investment slogan says that you "buy when there is blood in the streets." Markets that have had crises and collapses, such as South Korea in 1997, Russia in 1998, Iceland in 2008, and Greece in 2012, almost always have great returns within one to two years after the crash and crisis.

Ways to Invest in Turkey

There are two easy ways to invest in the country. iShares Turkey ETF (TUR NYSE) is the ETF. It peaked at $65 a share a few years ago and now trades around $42 after the recent devaluation of the Turkish lira (it was as low as $20 a few years ago). If Turkey follows the pattern of busts in Asia in the 1990s, Argentina in 2001, or Greece in 2012, the Turkish market could fall over 80% in U.S. dollar terms and this ETF into the single digits. It should be noted that a maximum pessimism bust does not have to see the market fall 90% (such as Brazil in 2016); many times they end with "only" a 60% or 70% decline. As TUR has already fallen about 70% in U.S. dollar terms, you might want to make a small first tranche investment and then wait for it to potentially fall more to invest more.

Another way to invest in Turkey is with Turkcell (TKC NYSE), the Turkish telecom company. In crises, I like to invest in telecom companies as proxies for the market. Here are the two reasons why:

1. Telecom companies have stable businesses. No matter how bad things get in the country, people are still going to use their cell phones, text, use the internet, and use telecommunications. Therefore, there will always be a large base and stream of income.
2. Most countries have one major telecom carrier that essentially has a monopoly in the country. With no main competition, it's difficult for these companies to fail even in a downturn.

Building the infrastructure for a telecom company is very expensive. These companies tend to have large amounts of debt, as they always need to keep improving technology and building infrastructure.

When there's a crisis in the country, the yield on interest rates spikes. As telecom companies tend to possess a large amount of debt, they tend to fall very hard. For example, during the 2001 crisis in Argentina, Telecom Argentina fell from a high of $20 to $0.50! Hellenic Telecom, the Greek telecom company, fell from north of $10 to under $1 a share in 2012. Both companies rallied strongly after their countries' crises. By 2007 Telecom Argentina was trading at a remarkable $25 a share. By mid-2013 Hellenic Telecom had rallied to nearly $7 a share.

Turkcell has fallen from north of $25 to $7 a share since 2007 (it has traded as low as $2.50). It is already beaten up and cheap, but could get cheaper if Turkey has an all-out crisis. The way I would invest in this company is by using a dollar-cost average system. This means to buy a little bit now and then buy more if Turkcell were to drop to under a dollar, like Hellenic Telecom and Telecom Argentina did.

Brazil

Brazil, like Turkey, had a huge boom after the financial crisis, and it issued a ton of debt in U.S. dollars. When there was QE and the Federal Reserve was buying low-yielding securities such as government bonds and mortgage-backed securities, it forced the private money into higher-risk and higher-yielding securities, one of these sectors being higher-yielding debt of foreign companies. Many companies in places like Brazil and Turkey offer yields two or three times higher than investment corporate grade bonds in the United States, and this obviously attracted capital. In addition, in the years following the financial crisis, the U.S. dollar was so weak, that made it even more attractive for these foreign companies to issue money in U.S. dollars, as their currencies were rising against the U.S. dollar.

There was some excitement in Brazil, as a right-wing president who was pro-business was elected in November of 2018. The problem is that Brazil is not in the same situation the United States was in 2016. The United States is the largest economy in the world and a global superpower, so when Trump was elected and changed policies to more pro-business, he had a lot of flexibility to do so and was not dependent on external forces. Brazil, on the other hand, is a natural resource–based economy, and much of its boom of the 2000s was based upon exporting resources and commodities to China. As the Chinese economy is slowing, this will probably have a negative impact on Brazil, more than anything that positive domestic policies can do for their economy. In the most recent election, the socialists regained power in Brazil.

Therefore, like Turkey, Brazil's currency could continue to weaken, making it more difficult for Brazilian companies to service foreign debt. However, like Turkey at some point, this could lead to a bottom and a lucrative buying opportunity.

Brazilian Stocks

iShares Brazil (EWZ NYSE) is the Brazilian ETF. It owns many of the large-cap companies in Brazil that make up the Bovespa, the Brazilian index. It should be noted that Brazil saw its first round of maximum pessimism back in 2015 and 2016, and the EWZ has more than doubled since then. I would be waiting for another decline in Brazilian stocks.

The major telecom company in Brazil is Telefonica Brazil (VIV NYSE). VIV trades at around $8 a share. This is an extremely cheap company possessing a low price-to-earnings ratio yielding over 6%! Because it is so cheap, I think you can put your toe into the water when buying this now and wait for a potentially lower price to average down. If there is a panic in Brazil and another market decline, this could be the type of stop that yields in the double digits, which is the type of thing that you haven't seen in the United States since the early 1980s.

Argentina

Argentina is an interesting country because I think it's a proxy for the rest of the world. In a way we are all becoming Argentine. There's a famous quote that when people look at Japan and Japan's lack of growth over the last 25 years, they say we're all becoming Japanese because many Western economies are now having problems with growing their economy, like Japan.

I think Argentina is maybe the best example of what all economies are becoming. If you look at Argentina's history over the last 35 years, it has strung together a series of booms and busts much like the United States and the rest of the Western world have since the 1990s. Many think Argentina has only seen collapses, but this is not true. Argentina has seen numerous crashes, including the late 1980s hyperinflation, 2001 financial crisis, and financial crisis of the last few years. However, after these crashes there have been huge booms. The year growth rate in the mid-1990s and early to mid-2000s in recovery after these crises was mostly in the double digits.

Argentina did not solve its problems of external debt, corruption, and socialism. This is part of the reason they go from bust to boom to bust to boom again. We have started to see that in the West since the 1990s. We had the tech bubble of the 1990s, the real estate bubble of the 2000s, and the everything bubble of the 2010s. In the developed world we have been stumbling from bubble to bubble and then from bust to bust like Argentina.

If Argentina has been a basket case for decades, why should it turn around? Enter Javier Milei. Milei is a rarity, a libertarian who was elected as the leader of a major country. Milei was a sign that the people of Argentina had had enough; he was elected on the premise of slashing spending, taxes, regulation, corruption, and the size of government. I would argue that no leader has been this drastic on the pro-capitalist side since World War II.

Margaret Thatcher and Ronald Reagan were pro-business, but they reformed within the confines of the mixed economy systems that were in place. Milei is ripping apart the system and starting a new one.

It should be noted that famed investor Stanley Druckenmiller bought a basket of Argentina stocks after watching Milei's pro-freedom, pro-capitalist speech at the World Economic Forum this past year. Druckenmiller said when he worked for Soros, if they saw a unique macro play, they would pay the play, then research later to see if they bought the right companies, and then adjust accordingly!

The good news for traders and speculators is that in a boom-bust economy there are great opportunities, especially for an investor who can buy during the bust and then sell during the boom and recovery.

Argentine Stocks

The Global X Argentina ETF (ARGT NYSE) is the Argentine ETF.

The telecom company in Argentina is Telefonica De Argentina (TEO NYSE). After crashing in 2001 to $0.50 a share, this ETF had a huge move, climbing $25 a share. It now trades about $7. It also pays a dividend of 2%. In addition, this company is battle seasoned, surviving many hyperinflations and meltdowns in the Argentine economy over the past 30 years.

I realize many Americans may cringe at the ticker of IRSA Inversiones y Representcns SA (IRS NYSE)! This IRS is investor friendly. IRS engages in diversified real estate activities in Argentina. It operates through five segments: shopping malls, offices, hotels, sales and developments, and others. The company is off from an all-time high of $30 and now trades at $16 (it was as low as $3 in 2020). It pays an incredible 11% dividend and has only a $1 billion market cap.

Argentina and India are probably my favorite long-term plays: Argentina due to its pro–free market policies and India due to its favorable demographics and long-term growth prospects.

GLOBAL REAL ESTATE—THE RISE OF PENTURBIA

In my first book, *Stock Market Panic!* published in 1998, I discussed a rise in a form of real estate called Penturbia. This is a shifting of real estate from large city centers and suburbs into smaller towns. I did this move in 2011 when I moved from Nassau, the large city in the Bahamas, to Eleuthera, a long, thin island that has a bunch of small towns. Eleuthera is more picturesque and has little to no traffic, cheaper real estate, less crime, and so on.

We will now really see the rise of Penturbia and smaller towns. It is already happening in the global economy and large cities affected by Covid and then for the current calls to defund police, and so on. There has already been huge demand for more rural real estate in the wake of this economic downturn. I suspect that island real estate that is isolated and rural areas in countries such as Australia and New Zealand will benefit, as will less-populated states such as Nevada, New Mexico, Wyoming, Montana, and so on. I see a long-term shift to Asia as being the economic center of the world, where real estate in urban centers will do well.

In addition, the economic backdrop to this shift to the penturbs or small centers makes sense from a demographic point of view; as the baby boomers retire, they will want to live in smaller centers, and as the Covid depression has changed spending habits, people will not be averse to live simpler lives in smaller population environments. I can tell you that prices here in Eleuthera where I live have exploded as people try to flee high taxes, crime, and problems that come with living in urban areas.

CONCLUSION

Emerging markets have underperformed during the 15-year era of near-zero rates and asset bubbles. However, they are still where the majority of the world's growth is. India and other Asian nations will continue to grow and do well in the coming years and decades. I love Argentina as a long-term turnaround play, as Milei moves the country from socialism to capitalism.

Finally, much of the Western world has seen huge real estate bubbles. I think in the coming years these bubbles will deflate or at least inflate at much slower levels, especially if interest rates rise in tandem with more problems with inflation.

6

New Tech: Artificial Intelligence, 3D Printing, and Fifth-Generation Wireless (5G)

One of the main investment themes in this book is that you want to stay away from sectors that are indebted: those that have benefited from financial hypernormalization and cheap money. While the Fed will try to inflate these bubbles by buying corporate debt, those bubbles are over. There is now a huge backlash against borrowing and buybacks, so many companies will begin to reduce debt in the coming years. On the consumer front, investors will be more frugal in the post-Covid world. This means less splurging on trips, expensive goods, and so on. Therefore, it is these sectors (e.g., large restaurant chains, airlines, hotel chains) that will struggle in the future.

What you want to do is find sectors and companies that are unleveraged (not operating on debt) and relatively inexpensive, that you identify as having optimistic future growth potential. Ideally, you want to find a sector that has some pre-existing growth and is not dependent on financial engineering. In Chapter 4, we looked at sectors that are inexpensive and beaten up. In the next three chapters, we will focus primarily on emerging sectors that have organic growth, such as new tech, cryptocurrencies and cannabis, and green energy.

Before we get to the latter of those sectors, I want to share with you three new tech sectors I have identified with great long-term prospects that are in the early stages of their booms: artificial intelligence, 3D printing, and fifth-generation wireless, or 5G. These technologies will change our life in the most profound of ways.

Throughout mankind's ascent over the last few hundred years, there has been a rapid rate of technological growth. In the 1800s, railroads changed the way the world traveled. In the 1920s, there were monster bull financial markets and advances in radio, electricity, and automobiles. In the 1980s and 1990s, there were booms in personal computer makers and companies that helped develop the internet. In the 2000s and 2010s, there were booms in companies that developed smartphones, the various apps for use on those devices that changed the fabric of society (gig workers and social media), and other wireless technology advances.

Three of the most interesting technologies going forward will be artificial intelligence, 3D printing, and the development of 5G and 6G networks. 5G has an interesting spin to the investment opportunity due to the backlash against Huawei and China, which was already starting pre-Covid, but now will pick up steam post-Covid. Additionally, other companies outside of China are paving the way in 5G technology, and I see them leading the way as countries shun Huawei and use more trusted providers. The United Kingdom already has such companies, attempting to become industry leaders in this advancing field and setting themselves apart from China.

ARTIFICIAL INTELLIGENCE (AI)

AI and robotics will disrupt the world as we know it. We are in the very early stages of infancy in these technologies. We've seen the weird-looking kangaroo metallic robots that deliver packages, the Amazon drones, and so on. What we fail to realize is that these robots are the equivalent of what the early-stage Commodore 64 and IBM mega-computers were to the computer manufacturing industry. In the future, AI won't just be robots, but highly complex systems that are able to solve problems, build products, and perform other functions without the absolute supervision and consistent oversight that current manufacturing machinery requires.

Research associated with AI is highly technical and specialized to each individual category of AI. The core problems of AI include programming computers for certain traits such as:

- Knowledge
- Reasoning
- Problem solving
- Perception
- Learning
- Planning
- Ability to manipulate and move objects

In the automobile sector, AI can help manufacture a car using purely robotics, then install software that can allow the car to drive itself without any human input. The driving system in the car will be able to find shortcuts, avoid areas of congestion, and even sense oncoming slowdowns in traffic, swerve, and avoid potential accidents. AI will replace manufacturing workers with the ability to assemble automobiles and other products much more precisely and efficiently. With people worried about being in tight spaces due to Covid, this might even accelerate the usage of robotics and AI throughout manufacturing sectors in the short term.

As stated previously, AI is very much in its infancy. Companies like IBM are developing supercomputers with AI potential; but there is no pure play that trades in the markets. The future of AI will be enormous. By some estimates, AI could lead to GDP growth of around 26%, or $22 trillion, by 2030. Mark Cuban has even been on record saying that the first person who can dominate the AI industry will be the world's first trillionaire.

With that being said, there are some companies with AI exposure. Sure, Amazon has its Alexa service, IBM has its Watson supercomputer, and even Blackberry is leading the way in autonomous technology for automobiles.

As I go to press, the company that is the AI favorite is Nvidia (NVDA NASDAQ), but as I discussed, the problems that Nvidia has are the complete overvaluation, euphoria, and parabola around the company. Super Micro Computer (SMCI NASDAQ) is another AI darling, but again the bubble has started to burst in this one. Figure 6.1 is the SOX index—the semiconductors, which are going parabolic just like they did during the 2000 tech bubble. The best time to buy the semis was in 2002 after that bubble burst. This is how I feel about them now. Let's let the first phase of the AI boom burst, then pick away at them afterward.

FIGURE 6.1 Semiconductor bubble.
Source: www.stockcharts.com

A CHEAP AI PLAY

As a percentage of its total business, Blackberry's autonomous automobile technology makes Blackberry (BB NYSE) the purest play on AI (they no longer make cell phones). Blackberry's QNX system is what it has developed to run automatic cars. QNX is based on the idea of running most of the operating system kernel in the form of several small tasks, known as resource managers. OEMs use QNX to power their instrument clusters, infotainment systems, and driver assistance systems that are available across numerous car brands, including Audi, BMW, Ford, Kia, Porsche, and Volkswagen. As recently as 2015, QNX tech was in 60 million vehicles. Blackberry still trades at a cheaper valuation, so it's an affordable price to pay to get some skin in the AI game.

Another characteristic of AI is the ability of a machine or computer to interface with your brain. At some point, the days of typing or speaking into your phone will be over. Some sort of software AI program will be able to project your thoughts into the phone and write or perform actions. Take Siri or Alexa, for example. Being able to link the human brain into a machine to do your bidding poses many moral and ethical questions, which create much of the criticism surrounding AI.

AI will disrupt and change your everyday life, from the way you live at home, to service and manufacturing jobs, to interfacing yourself with ultra-intelligent machines. Soon AI in both the manufacturing and automobile sectors will make the most immediate and important impact we see in our lives. Undoubtedly, it is bound to be a multi-trillion-dollar industry. As this technology continues to develop, I will certainly be on the lookout for more pure plays after the bubble bursts.

3D PRINTING

3D printing is the action or process of making a physical object from a three-dimensional digital model, typically by laying down many thin layers of a material in succession. The creation of a 3D, printed object is achieved using additive processes. In an additive process, an object is created by laying down successive layers of material until the object is created.

With everything else going on in the world, 3D printing has become a very underrated technology. With all the hype around autonomous cars, cryptocurrencies, and cloud computing, investors have almost forgotten about 3D printing. What makes 3D printing unique is that by laying down these materials in succession, it totally changes what we know as manufacturing today. Believe it or not, there are 3D printing machines that can print a house. Instead of having to first lay a foundation, nail down the flooring, put up walls, and then put on the roof, you put all the materials in the machine and the machine does this entire process at once.

3D printing can print shoes, toys, houses, and even human organs. During the Covid pandemic, 3D printing companies were printing swabs for testing. At some point, as the technology becomes cheaper and more efficient, it will change the nature of manufacturing. It will encourage companies to insource production rather than contracting out, and it will make us very flexible in terms of what we produce. Once a 3D printing machine becomes cheap enough for the average small business to purchase, that business will be able to customize its product, then manufacture in-house.

Even in the automobile sector, a joint venture between an Italian electric car company XEV and 3D printing company Polymaker has produced a 3D-printed car known as the LSEV. (The LSEV is a small two-seater smart car that will be 3D printed by these two companies and will retail for only $7,500.) 3D printing isn't one-dimensional (no pun intended).

I think another reason that 3D printing has been forgotten is that its bubble came earlier than the rest of the market. Most of the 3D printing stocks had huge gains from the end of the financial crisis in 2009 to 2014. Many of the stocks went parabolic and have crashed since. Therefore, with the 3D printers taking off nearly five years ago, many investors have forgotten about how exciting this technology really is.

3D Printing Stocks: The Sector Is Reminiscent of Past Bubbles and Busts

In 2014 many 3D printer stocks went parabolic. A parabolic curve (as discussed earlier) is a move in a stock or industry when the chart rises at an almost 90° angle. It's a very rare occurrence that happens near the end of bubbles. It happened in 1929 in the Dow Jones Industrial Average, 1980 in gold, and 1999 to 2000 in the NASDAQ. After these parabolic curves, the market crashes; then there are years of basing before the next bull market. Parabolic curves often occur early in an industry's or technology's life cycle, as there is a lot of hype and excitement over that industry or technology in its early years.

For example, in the 1929 bubble, a parabolic curve in stocks occurred during the first real boom in modern technology with the introduction of the automobile, radios, and other technologies. The commodities parabolic curve of the 1970s wasn't technology driven, but it was the first time the country had gone off the gold standard, which allowed unlimited amounts of printed money to slosh around. This in turn created the first ever blow-off in the price of real assets. The 1989 parabolic curve in Japan occurred as Japan became a technological and industrial power, and the market got way ahead of itself, overpricing the potential of Japan's prowess. The 1990s' NASDAQ parabolic curve saw the advent of fiber optics and the internet, with excitement surrounding those sectors.

Some bubbles and parabolic curves are one-off events, such as the South Sea bubble or Tulip Mania where the excitement in the sector causes it to blow off, crash, and never be heard from again. (Even then, these bubbles occurred during great booms in the United Kingdom and Holland, two global powers at the time, and were symptomatic of those booms.)

In the case of Japan, the valuations were so ridiculous (a block of real estate in Tokyo was worth the same as the entire state of California at the bubble top in 1989!). That is part of the reason Japan has not come back from its bubble nearly 30 years later. However, many bubbles usually base out for several years, and if the thesis is solid behind them, they can move higher and eventually trade to new highs. Gold broke its 1980 high in 2007. Even U.S. stocks, which melted down 89% during the Great Depression from 1929 to 1932, hit new highs 25 years later in 1954. Many of the quality technology stocks broke their 2000s high in the 2010s, 10 to 15 years after the dot-com bubble burst.

I expect that the 3D printing stocks will be like the bubbles that eventually traded to new highs, due to how dynamic the technology is. Now the valuations are solid in 3D printing stocks, and the long-term growth potential is spectacular.

3D Systems (DDD NYSE)

3D Systems, the first 3D printing stock I will look at, is the most well-known company in the sector. The company crashed to about $2 a share during the 2008–2009 financial crisis, then soared as 3D printing stocks went on a frenzy into 2014, blowing off to nearly $100 a share! The stock crashed to just over $3 a share in 2024. The stock now possesses a decent valuation. In 2014, at the top for 3D printing stocks, the company was trading over 10 times revenues. It now trades at around 0.9 times revenues.

A potential kicker for DDD is that the FDA recently approved the 3D printing of dentures. As baby boomers age, they will need to replace teeth and other dental work. This is estimated to be a $4 billion market by 2030. As I write, DDD has about $450 million in annual sales. If they could, say, just get 25% of this market ($1 billion) by 2030, that would cause revenues to explode and help the stock rebound.

Trading south of $3 a share as I write, this stock represents good value, and I would use the same dollar-cost averaging strategy I have recommended all throughout this book to purchase this stock. This being to purchase a bit here and more if it falls more in a market decline.

Stratasys (SSYS NASDAQ)

This is the other leading stock in the 3D printing arena. Their revenues are about $670 million. Due to the struggles DDD has had, SSYS has a slightly higher market cap of $600 billion versus $350 million for DDD. This stock collapsed from over $140 a share to $9 in 2024. What's interesting is during that collapse from 2015 to the present, revenues at the company had stayed flat! This means the stock has gone from trading nearly 14 times revenues to over 1 time revenues.

The company does not have a debt problem, as it has only $18 million of long-term debt and has over $160 million cash on its balance sheet. Therefore, while both DDD and SSYS lose money, I do not see any chance of them going under. Their growth has stagnated after the initial boom phase from 2009 to 2014. Due to the potential in the industry, at some point growth will resume.

Like DDD, SSYS represents decent value at current levels. As with DDD, I would buy a small amount of SSYS at current prices; then if there is a bear market in equity markets, which drags the 3D printing stocks lower with them, add to those positions at lower prices.

Organovo (ONVO NASDAQ)

Organovo is a unique 3D printer that is made not by an industrial company but by a medical company. They print organs and other internal body parts that can be used in surgery. This is a very high-risk/high-reward company. Either they'll be successful and be able to convert 3D printing into the medical realm or they won't. The stock has collapsed like everything else in the sector from over $270 a share to $0.76 a share. This is the type of stock that will either go to zero or go up 20, 30, or 50 times in value. There will probably be no in-between. With ONVO down to the penny stock range and a market cap of only $35 million as I go to press, I think it's worth a shot here as a high-risk speculation.

FIFTH-GENERATION WIRELESS

Fifth-generation wireless (5G) is the latest iteration of cellular technology, engineered to greatly increase the speed and responsiveness of wireless networks. 5G will also enable a sharp increase in the amount of data transmitted over wireless systems, due to more available bandwidth and advanced antenna technology.

5G promises mobile data speeds that far outstrip the fastest home broadband network currently available to consumers. With speeds of up to 100 gigabits per second, 5G is set to be as much as 100 times faster than 4G.

One of the reasons 5G is in the news now is because the United States is very behind in the development of the technology and will almost definitely have to use a foreign provider to implement 5G. One of the leaders in the technology is a large Chinese company, Huawei. However, Huawei is a private company closely associated with the Chinese government. Therefore, foreign governments and investors outside of China worry about Huawei using their access to networks for the storage of information and whether the Chinese government has backdoor access to information.

If many countries decide not to use Huawei's 5G technology due to privacy issues and its association with the communist government in China, will there be opportunities that arise from this geopolitical issue with this new technology?

I think that it is two old names that might benefit from this new technology and the privacy issues that exist with Huawei.

Ericsson (ERIC NASDAQ) and Nokia (NOK NYSE)

Ericsson and Nokia were two of the leading headset and cell phone makers in the 1990s and 2000s before the introduction of the iPhone and Android smartphones and the rise of Apple and Samsung. With their smartphone business decimated, these two companies have had to reinvent themselves. They now operate digital networks and services for much of their business and revenues.

Both have been focusing on the development of 5G technology to compete with Huawei. The advantage these companies have when compared to Huawei is purely political. Ericsson is Swedish and Nokia is Finnish. Countries that are known for sweets, democratic socialism, vodka, hockey, and bikini models. These are not exactly countries that incite fear or have major opponents or enemies on an international geopolitical level.

Nokia is an interesting company because they are also re-expanding into cell phones. If you are old enough, you will remember the Nokia 3310. This was the tough cookie of cell phones that was almost impossible to break. Nokia then bungled the market, not realizing how popular the iPhone would be, and their Lumia Windows phone was a disaster as no one wanted to be on a Windows operating system for a cell phone. Nokia now is producing effective low-cost cell phones and has 2.2% of the cell phone market.

As most of their new phones are lower cost (which is what sells in emerging markets), it gives another potential kicker to Nokia. As stated, if being associated with China bothers you, Nokia makes these phones in Finland and Hungary.

Many countries may use Nokia and Ericsson for their 5G rollouts, as there is no fear of being spied on by the Chinese communist government. Both companies recently received a boost when Japanese mobile carrier SoftBank named Nokia and Ericsson as flagship equipment providers for its 5G deployment.

Ericsson is also in talks to provide 5G in India. Geopolitically, India and China do not get along, and they will be more at ease using Ericsson over Huawei. 5G is estimated to have $27 billion in revenue opportunities to telecom providers in India alone by 2030.

In a report by Ovum titled, "5G Economics of Entertainment Report," it is forecast that over the period of 2019 to 2028, "media and entertainment companies will be competing to win a share of a near-$3 trillion cumulative wireless revenue opportunity.

Experiences enabled by 5G networks will account for nearly half of this revenue opportunity (close to $1.3 trillion)."*

Due to their loss in market share in the mobile market over the last 15 years, Ericsson and Nokia have both been in restructuring mode as they shifted toward networking and services businesses. The 5G opportunity could turn them around and return them to prominence, especially if for political reasons many countries shun Huawei for Ericsson and Nokia.

The two companies have a combined $60 billion market cap. Both are over 90% below their dot-com bubble tops of 2000. Ericsson is 40% below its prefinancial crisis highs of 2007 and Nokia 80% below its 2007 highs. If they can just grasp a small share of the 5G market going forward, it could be worth in the tens if not hundreds of billions for them—it would drive these companies back to prominence.

5G as the Catalyst for Ericsson and Nokia

One of the aspects you must understand about trading maximum pessimism is you usually need a catalyst to turn around the company. After the dot-com bust, Apple was beaten up and cheap, but it had been for years with no real catalyst to turn the company around. In 2003 Apple was trading nearly 80% off its all-time highs.

The turnaround for Apple was the iPod and then the iTunes store, which gave it revenue generators. Tata Motors, which I talked about earlier, needed a catalyst when it was $3.50 a share. The catalyst was Tata's purchase of Land Rover and Jaguar, which gave it two brand names in the luxury car market. When luxury sales in the 2010s rebounded globally, it drove the stock higher. With Ericsson

* Source: https://www.intc.com/news-events/press-releases/detail/119/intel-study-finds-5g-will-drive-1-3-trillion-in-new

and Nokia, we see a specific turnaround catalyst, this being their entrance into the potential growth of the 5G market.

A Special Maximum Pessimism Streaming Play—FuboTV Inc.,TV (FUBO NYSE)

A company I really like is FuboTV. This is a streaming company that went public in 2018 with a niche of broadcasting Premier League Football (or what Americans call soccer). I am a huge soccer fan, and it is probably my second favorite sport next to American football (I played goalie when I was a kid). FuboTV has expanded, implementing regular cable packages and other sports packages, even making deals with the NBA and MLB for exclusive coverage on individual teams.

In early 2024 FOX, CBS, and Disney announced they wanted to do a sports package called Venu. For years FuboTV had been asking these companies for permission to do a "skinny package" where they just offer sports, but these networks kept rejecting their offer. After they announced the launch of Venu, FuboTV then put in an injunction charging these companies with antitrust violations. In August of 2024 a New York judge agreed to the injunction and set the antitrust case for October of 2025. Even the Venu logo looks like a rip-off from Fubo's!

On top of this, FuboTV has seen strong growth. Revenues are growing at nearly 20% a year, and it trades at roughly a $550 million market cap with nearly $1.6 billion in yearly sales. They still lose money but say they will be cash flow positive and profitable by 2026.

When you invest in maximum pessimism, you also want a catalyst for a company or industry. When John Templeton put on his famous trade of 1939 when he invested in 100 companies trading under $1 a share, his catalyst was that the war effort would drive demand for goods and services as the United States supplied the Allies war effort and this demand would turn around the economy.

As we were just about to go print on this book, FuboTV has made a deal with Disney. This deal gives Disney 70% ownership of FuboTV and also Disney, ESPN, Fox, and others agree to pay FuboTV $220 million in cash to resolve the antitrust suit. In addition, FuboTV will act as a live-streaming service arm of Disney with this deal and probably be given access to their live sporting events.

This news caused FuboTV to spike from $1.45 a share to over $5 a share. This is one example of how maximum pessimism works. Buy an asset that is cheap and undervalued with a potential catalyst and it will probably work out!

CONCLUSION

In this chapter we looked at future technologies. At the moment the technology that is all the rage is AI. Many of the leading AI stocks (mostly semiconductors) are in massive bubbles and not really worth buying. I have given a cheap AI play in the former cell phone powerhouse Blackberry, which now is going into automotive AI technologies. We also take our unique approach to 3D printing, which was a bubble way back in 2014 and now is beaten up and cheap. We see the technology still growing and catalysts going for these companies (such as 3D printing of dentures) in the coming years. Finally, we also look at 5G, moving into super-high-speed data networks. It is also a growth industry; two former Nordic cell phone giants (Nokia and Ericsson) are the Western leaders in 5G networks, and Nokia gives you a cell phone kicker to boot!

7

Crypto and Cannabis

Crypto and cannabis are two interesting sectors because they have both seen stretches of exponential growth early on in their respective industry's growth cycle, followed by those bubbles each bursting. In 2017, the cryptocurrency sector saw a parabolic rise followed by a huge burst; the same occurred in the cannabis industry the following year, in 2018. However, I now think that these sectors are near their nadir, and you can find great opportunities in these underappreciated areas as they turn around.

THE RISE OF CRYPTOCURRENCY AND DIGITAL ASSETS

In recent years, we have seen growing interest within the cryptocurrency sector. A cryptocurrency, or "crypto" for short, is a digital asset class consisting of peer-to-peer transactions (no financial middleman or banking intermediary necessary). These transactions are verified and controlled by cryptography. Crypto projects tend to be open source, allowing other developers to revise the code to create a new crypto as a slightly different offshoot from the previous crypto. This adaptability, constant improvement, and open collaboration between many projects emboldens the crypto asset class with the ability to fulfill potentially unlimited uses. Today, there are countless cryptocurrencies, with more and more being created every day. The first of which and most well known is Bitcoin.

Bitcoin was launched in the aftermath of the financial crisis of 2008 by its unknown creator(s) under the pseudonym of Satoshi Nakamoto. The idea and mechanics of Bitcoin can be found in the white paper titled "Bitcoin: A Peer-to-Peer Electronic Cash System" that was released on October 31, 2008. We saw the launch of the Bitcoin network on January 3, 2009, when Satoshi mined the first Bitcoin block of the blockchain, known as genesis block, Block 0. There was a message left by Satoshi in this block reading, "The Times 03/Jan/2009 Chancellor on brink of second bailout for banks," the headline of a *London Times* article released that day, suggesting it was Satoshi's solution to the many problems associated with fractional-reserve banking and the extraordinary risks involved when greed overshadows financial logic.

Cemented in the Bitcoin blockchain forever, this note is described as one of the most secure documents in history. Many people and groups around the world have been on a quest to uncover the pseudonymous creator of this revolutionary new asset. Although the identity of Satoshi Nakamato is likely to never be known with complete certainty, that is much less important than the gift they have given to the world. For the first time ever, people have the ability to completely control their money.

Cryptos provide some benefits over traditional paper money (fiat) and government-controlled currencies. Some of the benefits include borderless payments, significantly cheaper fees, no sending limits, near-instant send times, no middleman or trusted third party, enhanced privacy, superior security, and transparency. You can access your funds from anywhere as long as you have your private key. Bitcoin cannot be counterfeited and is created by a process called mining. This process involves people from all around the world connecting their computers to the Bitcoin network. Their computers run an algorithm involving incredibly advanced mathematics that verifies and confirms the individual transactions, which are bundled in blocks sent over the blockchain network. Once a computer running the algorithm has solved the equation, the block is finalized with all the transactions that occurred during the mining process, that block is added to the previously mined block, and the blockchain grows one block longer. In return for the work their computers are doing, the miner that solves the equation is rewarded with new Bitcoin.

Every transaction since the launch of the Bitcoin network is recorded in a public ledger known as the blockchain. There is a set mining schedule to release Bitcoin (BTC) into circulation. In the beginning, the reward for mining a block was 50 BTC and the reward halves every 210,000 blocks until all 21 million BTC are in circulation. On May 11, 2020, the reward was halved again, from 12.5 down to 6.25. The last Bitcoin is expected to be mined into circulation around the year 2140.

Bitcoin has a fixed supply that cannot be manipulated by governments, banks, or any malevolent actor. This alone makes it a great addition to any portfolio as a hedge against the depreciation of traditional currencies. The transparent supply is attractive since it solves the problem of inflationary fears. Due to Bitcoin being a very secure store of value, many see it as a form of "digital gold." There are many arguments for both Bitcoin and gold. Historically, gold has been a very trusted safe haven asset; it has withstood the test of time, and there is the argument it will likely outlast any man-made currency due to its intrinsic elemental value and natural scarcity. It also doesn't rely on the internet. The actual supply, however, is uncertain, and it's more difficult to transfer. With Bitcoin, you can send any amount of funds across the globe within minutes. Digital tokens backed by physical gold may eventually solve this problem. In the future, we will likely see a lot of physical assets and commodities that are backed (secured) by digital tokens. Money, and the way people make transactions, is evolving as the world becomes more digital day by day.

As an investment, Bitcoin has made headlines several times, most often stemming from its volatility. Like most new technological innovations, Bitcoin lends itself to boom-and-bust cycles: first starting as a low-volume emerging market, to the block reward halving schedule serving as a supply shock for the amount being added into circulation, followed by more and more public acceptance and awareness, leading to mainstream investor confidence. We have seen four crashes and several major corrections in Bitcoin's short lifetime (as a counterpoint, the euro is only slightly older than Bitcoin, having launched in January 1999), most recently in the lead up to the great crypto crash of 2018. After a run of about 2,700% in 2017, Bitcoin reached a high of $19,891, securing its place as one of the largest speculative bubbles in history alongside Tulip Mania and the dot-com bubble. (See Table 7.1.)

TABLE 7.1 Bitcoin (BTC) historical corrections

Correction Period ≥ 30%						
Correction Start Date	Correction End Date	#Days in Correction	Bitcoin High Price	Bitcoin Low Price	% Decline	$ Decline
12 Jan 2012	27 Jan 2012	16	$7.38	$3.80	–49%	–$3.58
18 Aug 2012	19 Aug 2012	3	$16.41	$7.10	–57%	–$9.31
6 Mar 2013	7 Mar 2013	2	$49.17	$33.00	–33%	–$16.17
21 Mar 2013	23 Mar 2013	3	$76.91	$50.09	–35%	–$26.82
10 Apr 2013	12 Apr 2013	3	#259.34	$45.00	–83%	–$214.34
19 Nov 2013	19 Nov 2013	1	$755.00	$378.00	–50%	–$377.00
30 Nov 2013	14 Jan 2015	411	$1,163.00	$152.40	–87%	–$1,010.60
10 Mar 2017	25 Mar 2017	16	$1,350.00	$891.33	–34%	–$458.67
25 May 2017	27 May 2017	3	$2,760.10	$1,850.00	–33%	–$910.10
12 Jun 2017	16 Jul 2017	35	$2,980.00	$1,830.00	–39%	–$1,150.00
2 Sep 2017	15 Sep 2017	14	$4,979.90	$2,972.01	–40%	–$2,007.89
8 Nov 2017	12 No 2017	5	$7,888.00	$5,555.55	–30%	–$2,332.45
17 Dec 2017	2 Feb 2018	48	$19,666.00	$8,094.80	–59%	–$11,571.20

MICROSTRATEGY (MSTR)—POSTER CHILD FOR THE CURRENT CRYPTO BOOM

Just like Nvidia is the poster child for the tech and everything bubble, I think the poster child for this phase of the crypto boom (there were also booms in 2017 and 2021) is Microstrategy. This is the company that was founded by Michael Saylor and was one of the darlings of the dot-com boom. The stock had a massive blow-off in 2000, collapsed, and did not hit those highs until it became a market darling again, this time during the crypto boom. Microstrategy is properly named, as it has a strategy of borrowing money and then using it to buy bitcoin. Using debt to buy bitcoin leverages the company even more. As you can see in Figure 7.1, Microstrategy has had a monster run, which took out the 2000 high and more. I feel that just as Microstrategy was one of the poster children of the dot-com boom and bust of 2000, it will again be a poster child for the crypto boom and bust of 2024–2025 and beyond!

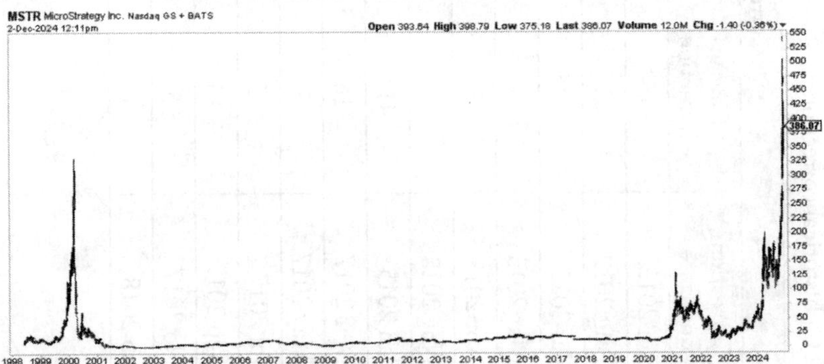

FIGURE 7.1 Microstrategy boom, bust, and boom of 1998–2024.
Source: www.stockcharts.com

Also, Figure 7.2 is a chart of Bitcoin that shows the booms and busts of the last 10 years. Bitcoin has traded only since 2009, so Bitcoin traded only during this entire huge asset bubble. In 2018,

2020, and 2022, when the market saw short-term bear markets (with the S&P 500 dropping nearly 20% in 2018 and nearly 30% in 2020 and 2022), Bitcoin dropped nearly 80% in 2018 and 2022 and nearly 65% in 2020. But we don't know how Bitcoin will react in a longer-term bear market. I feel it will fall with the NASDAQ rather than being some sort of "store of value" or "flight to safety."

FIGURE 7.2 Bitcoin booms and busts from 2009 to the present.
Source: www.stockcharts.com

THE RISE OF BITCOIN AND ETHEREUM

Several factors resulted in the dramatic rise in price in 2017. Growth of interest led to more mainstream media coverage, increasing the inflow of cash. Even suspected market manipulation involves USDT (Tether), a U.S. dollar stable coin with a token supply that can be increased or printed with added U.S. dollar backing. Ethereum, another relatively new token, gained popularity with the ability to process smart contracts on blockchain, expanding the use case of blockchain beyond currency.

We saw hundreds of projects create their own tokens on the Ethereum blockchain. The problem with this was that the Ethereum network they launched on at that time could only process under 30 transactions per second. For any of these projects to become more than just vaporware, they would have had to be able to scale to thousands of transactions per second, which simply wasn't possible at that time. With all these newly launched tokens, everyone was on the hunt to find the next hot thing. Initial coin offerings (ICOs) to sell their tokens or coins became popular, and money was flowing in. This is where we see similarities to the dot-com bubble. Most of these coins didn't even have a working product! Some companies with nothing to do with blockchain were even adding blockchain to their names and seeing a surge in stock price. It was a frenzy.

As we know, market cycles exist, and nothing can go up forever. In the early days of cryptocurrency, there was a lack of regulation and insufficient security measures to protect investors. The rapid growth in the crypto space attracted many bad actors. Numerous ICOs turned out to be scams, exchanges were hacked, and many individuals fell victim to phishing and other scams. In the "wild west" of crypto in 2017, fortunes could be made or lost in a day. Volatility increased with fears of regulation by the U.S. Securities and Exchange Commission (SEC), government bans, and crackdowns. The bubble eventually burst in January 2018, coinciding with the launch of the first cash-settled Bitcoin futures contract, which allowed mainstream investors to speculate on future prices and short the market with heavy volume. Bitcoin continued to lose over 80% of its value in 2018, a decline worse than the dot-com bubble.

Following the 2018 crash, the market settled down, but coding and building continued, establishing a lot of necessary infrastructure. Cryptos started with Bitcoin, initially working only as a new form of currency. In addition, the price bottomed and then soared to nearly $70,000 a coin in 2021 and $100,000 2024.

Almost everything we do can run on this cutting-edge technology. Early on, transactions were too slow for mainstream adoption. Could you imagine waiting 20 minutes to pay for a cup of coffee at Starbucks? Years later, cryptos can now send transactions just as fast as, if not faster than, a credit card swipe. The traditional banking system has always felt threatened by this technology, and never more so than now. Who will want to use banks when they can safely store their own money and send it instantly without fees?

At the same time, we are seeing similarities to the early days of the dot-com era. One of the first major use cases emerging with this promising new technology is online gambling and sports betting. Currently, the online gaming industry generates roughly $50 billion yearly and is steadily growing. This was one of the first industries to gain traction and achieve mass adoption in the early days of the internet. We are now witnessing a similar trend unfold on blockchain since transaction speeds are now near instant and capable of handling thousands of transactions per second. Several key advantages draw users to these platforms over traditional websites. First, games built on crypto networks are probably fair and transparent. For example, in online poker, backend data is encrypted so that no users can see other players' cards, eliminating scandals that have occurred on traditional websites in the past. Such scandals have caused users to lose millions of dollars unfairly. Several projects are targeting this profitable market. The cryptocurrency landscape is constantly evolving, with new use cases emerging and transforming the way we interact with digital assets. As blockchain technology advances, the applications of cryptocurrencies extend far beyond their original purpose as a medium of exchange, encompassing areas such as decentralized finance (DeFi), nonfungible tokens (NFTs), gaming, supply chain management, tokenization of real-world assets, AI integration, travel, and more.

In travel, we see companies like Travala, which accept many different forms of payment but offer discounts to those who pay in Travala's native token (AVA). They currently offer accommodations at over 500,000 properties in over 200 countries and plan to scale up to at least 1.5 million properties. The platform's token allows for various incentives and discounts, such as earning rewards from holding the currency or spending it directly on travel. Tokens can be locked on the platform in tiers of a smart program to earn rewards in the form of AVA or BTC givebacks on bookings. The earned tokens can then be used on the platform or sold on an exchange, giving users flexibility.

DeFi applications continue to emerge. For example, Fideum (FI) aims to serve as a comprehensive banking solution by integrating traditional financial services with blockchain technology, making them more accessible, secure, and efficient through its suite of services and strategic partnerships. They currently have a partnership with Mastercard to enhance financial infrastructure and services for retail and institutional clients.

In DeFi, noncustodial options like Chainflip (FLIP) are gaining popularity. Chainflip operates in a fully decentralized manner, removing the need for centralized exchanges that can be prone to hacks, fraud, and operational downtimes. By leveraging decentralized protocols, they ensure that users retain full control of their assets throughout the swapping process, enhancing security and trust. Chainflip's architecture is designed for high-speed transactions, enabling quick execution of cross-chain swaps. The use of automated smart contracts ensures that transactions are processed efficiently, often within minutes, providing a user experience that rivals, and in some cases exceeds, that of traditional centralized exchanges. Chainflip also enhances interoperability by allowing seamless transfers of assets between different blockchain networks. This flexibility enables users to move their assets freely and interact with a wide range of decentralized applications (dApps) across multiple ecosystems without being confined to a single blockchain.

Speed and scalability are always crucial in the crypto sector. Telos (TLOS) is pioneering a fully decentralized protocol aimed at significantly enhancing the scalability, efficiency, and cost-effectiveness of zero-knowledge proofs (ZKPs) on blockchain networks. SNARKtor is a cutting-edge blockchain technology that uses ZKPs to allow users to prove they know something without revealing any details about it. Imagine you have a secret, like a password, and you want to show someone you know it without telling them what it is. Or the game of Battleship, where you can know if your move is a hit without having to trust your opponent to tell you. SNARKtor makes this possible in a fast, secure, and efficient way, allowing for private transactions and data verification on the blockchain without compromising privacy or security. These transactions can settle nearly instantly with new hardware-accelerated approaches. This technology can be used in many fields, such as finance, health care, and digital identity, to ensure that sensitive information stays private while still being verified accurately.

Finally, I like to issue a warning on the Bitcoin ETF. Many in the crypto universe believe this is the ultimate acceptance by the mainstream and a sign Bitcoin is entering the mainstream and will launch to the upside as the demand from the ETF drives the price higher. As I write in September 2024, huge inflows into the Bitcoin ETF have not driven the Bitcoin price higher. In 2006 many of us in the precious metals industry thought the introduction of the GDX and GDXJ gold equity ETFs would bring a similar boom to gold equities. However, they did the opposite; instead of bringing in long-term investors, they brought in weak hands.

Before the introduction of these ETFs, most retail investors in precious metals equities were long-term buyers of gold equities just like the HODLrs of the Bitcoin universe. The ETFs, though, brought in more of the trading types and "weak hands" that would be shaken out on any decline. When gold fell in the mid-2010s, the holders of the ETFs sold, and this caused the ETFs to sell gold equities and led to over a decade-long period of underperformance.

As just mentioned, the introduction of Bitcoin ETFs has not moved the price upward in 2024, and when there is some sort of correction or bear market in the crypto market, I feel the "weak hands" will dump and it could lead to a period of underperformance in Bitcoin. In addition, most studies have shown that Bitcoin has a much higher correlation with tech stocks, the NASDAQ, and "risk on" assets rather than being a currency hedge. If the stock market plummets and the everything bubble bursts, I expect Bitcoin will fall with these "risk on" assets. I do feel a large drawdown in Bitcoin would bring a great buying opportunity, but I would not chase it at the near-$100,000 Bitcoin trades at as I write this chapter in 2024.

CANNABIS

At one point in 2017 and 2018, this was one of the hottest sectors of the market, and it is a warning about buying into hype and bubbles. The hype around cannabis started 12 or 13 years ago when certain states in the United States began to legalize it. That was the early stage of the bull market. At that time there were a lot of very dubious penny stock–type companies that were in the cannabis sector. The game really changed when Canada legalized cannabis. This made it the first sovereign nation in the developed world to legalize cannabis.

Canada came up with a very specific set of rules for production regulation and distribution. As Canada is a leading country for venture capital for small caps through the mining industry, the infrastructure was there to raise money for cannabis deals. In addition, many American companies cannot list on the NYSE because cannabis is still illegal at the federal level. As a result., the Canadian Stock Exchange (CSE) became the leading stock exchange for these cannabis companies and a way for Americans to get in on these stocks.

Cannabis Bubble 1.0 in 2018

In 2017 and 2018 Canada was in a cannabis frenzy. Being Canadian and traveling back every so often from the Bahamas, I can tell you I saw it firsthand. Everyone and their brother and sister had a cannabis deal. I visited numerous greenhouses, plants, and other facilities that were about to grow cannabis. Valuations were extremely stretched, and they blew off and crashed. At the time, I felt the cannabis market was like the internet stocks in the late 1990s. If you remember in the late 1990s, many internet stocks were trading at ridiculous valuations, discounting years or even decades of growth. We saw a similar phenomenon in the cannabis sector in 2018. Many of the Canadian cannabis companies were trading at 20 or 30 times revenues, discounting growth into 2020 to 2022 or even 2025 as production came online. (Note: This growth never came.)

We have discussed parabolic charts many times in this book. Cannabis was an example of this. Figure 7.3 shows a chart for Canopy Growth, which for a time was the largest cannabis company in the world; this was the darling of the cannabis bubble in Canada in 2017 to 2018. They even received an investment from giant Constellation Brands (STZ NYSE, which owns Robert Mondavi wines and Corona beer) in 2017. In 2022 Constellation Brands had to write off this investment to the tune of a $1.1 billion loss, showing even the best and brightest can make mistakes. Canopy Growth spiked from $4 to nearly $550 from 2015 to 2018 and now trades back at $4! Parabolic curves die hard!

FIGURE 7.3 Canopy Growth parabolic curve boom and bust!
Source: www.stockcharts.com

Canadian companies, being the first to the sector, masked the problem they will run into as a sector matures: that the cost of production in Canada is high compared to other jurisdictions. Due to the weather in Canada, most of the production must be hydroponics, greenhouse, or indoor production. However, if you're producing in South America, the Caribbean, or countries with better weather, you can produce outdoors, which is much cheaper. In addition, the cost of labor and other costs such as energy are cheaper in other countries. Therefore, while Canadian producers were the first to produce, they may be replaced by lower-cost producers going forward.

In addition, like the dot-com bubble, almost everything has crashed as the cannabis bubble burst. Even the best companies will fall 80% or 90% in value. The good news is there is now value in the sector. In addition, we have a potential catalyst. Many of these companies have operations in the United States as well, and many states are starting to legalize cannabis. Costs of operations are lower in the United States, and the market is nearly 10 times larger.

While I feel many of the Canadian producers could fail, the two I think will be fine long term are Aurora Cannabis (ACB NYSE) and Cronos Group (CRON NASDAQ). Aurora and Cronos are two leaders that have received large investments from

U.S. multinationals. Aurora has also expanded operations into the United States and Germany (which recently legalized as well). In addition, Aurora, while it has diluted its stock, has raised millions in recent years to pay down its debt. The company is virtually debt free now.

For those looking at long-term investments, I think it is time to start to edge in, as the companies are so beat up. Foreign producers will also have an upper hand in terms of exporting to the U.S. and European markets as they legalize, due to their lower cost of production and therefore a lower-cost product. It is companies and properties in these regions that I will be watching after a potential bear market in cannabis stocks.

The issue in the short term for cannabis legalization in the United States will be the recent U.S. election. The Democrats were much more open to legalizing cannabis than the Republicans. With the Republicans controlling all three branches of the government for at least two years, I do not see much happening on the cannabis front. It is true that they are now allowed to do business with U.S. banks, which will help them in the states where cannabis is legal. However, federal legalization is still much more important for growth in this sector.

Many cannabis equities fell hard after the election. In Florida, legalization was rejected, mostly because the right to sell cannabis was going to go to a few companies. This would limit competition and cause the few companies to sell at higher prices.

In the hilarious Canadian movie *Trailer Park Boys: Don't Legalize It*, the character Ricky, one of the characters from the TV show *Trailer Park Boys* (your author's favorite TV show), goes to the Canadian parliament to protest the legalization of cannabis. He gives a hilarious speech telling the members of parliament they will screw it up like they screw everything else up! Ricky was 100% correct; the Canadian legalization was a disaster with high costs, stagnant sales, and huge losses for the cannabis companies which led to the cannabis equities collapsing in price.

Part of the cannabis sector you will want to look at companies involved in the marketing and development of certain cannabis products and brands. In any boom, marketing is extremely important. After Prohibition, brands such as Busch, Budweiser, and Coors and foreign products such as Heineken, Guinness, Dom Perignon, and Moet succeeded due to branding. They became household names. Beer wasn't just beer, champagne wasn't just champagne; people wanted these brands and the quality associated with them. Firms that help brand cannabis and take a percentage of the revenue will succeed in the sector going forward. Long term, the sector is exciting and will see growth. The sector is estimated to have north of $40 billion in revenues by 2030.

CONCLUSION

Crypto and cannabis are on the opposite ends of the spectrum right now. As I write in the fall of 2024, Bitcoin is nearing $100,000 and looks like it is going to see a blow-off similar to 2017 and 2021, which means we could see a large decline if there is a bear market in equities and risk assets in the coming years. I do believe that Bitcoin is an excellent risk on trade; where I disagree with coiners is that it is a "store of value or currency hedge." Bitcoin has a high correlation with the NASDAQ not trading counter the U.S. dollar or acting as a currency hedge. In addition, we have never seen how Bitcoin and crypto will act in a prolonged bear market. Bitcoin began to trade in 2009 during a 15-year bull market in risk assets where the drawdowns in asset markets were short-lived.

Cannabis is on the flip side of the coin. The cannabis sector saw its bubble burst in 2018, and most of the stocks are down 95% or more. The real driver for these stocks will be federal legalization, as the United States is the largest and still most potentially profitable market. As there will be no federal legalization within the next few years, I think you can remain patient on the cannabis stocks. But at some point they will represent excellent value.

8

Green Energy and Rare Earth Metals

With rapid advances in technology and an increased environmental awareness on the global scale, renewable or "green" energy sources and the mining of rare earths and precious metals are two rapidly expanding areas of the economy. A renewed interest in global warming and climate change, along with the pressure for governments and businesses to become more environmentally friendly, makes looking into these sectors of the market an obvious move.

The Green New Deal, introduced by Alexandria Ocasio-Cortez along with other members of Congress, brought the green movement to the forefront of the world stage. However, with an increased awareness, it also has shown just how expensive it would be to convert into a fully "green" future. The cost of the Green New Deal has been projected at $90 trillion over the span of a decade. Currently, the economy in the United States is valued at about $27 trillion. This illustrates just how large of a shift this would be, and that's if the proposed plan stays within budget! All the bailouts and spending due to the Covid-19 recession have been approximately $5 trillion to date, and we can see how hard this has stressed our economy. This proposed Green New Deal would cost almost double that annually for the entire 10 years! This Green New Deal, presented to create sustainability, seems unsustainable.

One thing I have learned in my 20 years of investing and trading in markets is that the gloom-and-doom outlook predicting an end-of-the-world scenario may sell books, but these prophecies are rarely grounded in fact or end up coming to fruition.

When I began investing, two books that I read really resonated with me in the gloom-and-doom department. The first book was *Bankruptcy 1995* by Harry Figgie. This book's basic premise was that due to the expansion in the government deficit, the government would be bankrupt by the mid-1990s. Figgie's main predication *has* come true, and the government debt is even higher than where he predicted it would be in 2020. However, due to numerous financial bubbles and juggling of debt, moving and ultra-low interest rates, and federal buyouts, we've managed to avoid bankruptcy. The second book, *The Great Reckoning* by James Dale Davidson, was published in 1994. It had a similar thesis to *Bankruptcy 1995*, being that the Western world was taking on too much debt and at some point would enter a debt crisis in the not-so-distant future. This inevitably led up to what Davidson referred to as "The Great Reckoning."

Let me state that these two individuals were not wrong in their basic belief that the world was taking on too much debt. It's no secret that governments around the world possess record debt levels they've never seen before en masse. However, throughout all of this, due to financial engineering, QE, and other factors, governments around the world are still solvent and rates are still low.

Global warming alarmists are doing the same gloom-and-doom fear mongering, just from an environmental standpoint rather than an economic one. In 1989, when some of the first reports on global warming began to surface, they said that the world would enter a crisis by the year 2000, which did not occur. Al Gore in his movie

An Inconvenient Truth predicted that the water levels would rise in many parts of the earth and much of that land would be underwater by 2016. Glacier Park in Montana recently had to remove signs that stated the glaciers in the park would not exist by 2020 or 2030 due to man-made climate change, because the glaciers are in fact not receding! None of these extreme gloom-and-doom scenarios have come to pass. Therefore, I take the end-of-the-world climate alarmists with a grain of salt and choose to not make my financial decisions based on such predictions.

I do see a diversification of energy usage across the board as green energy technologies, such as solar power and wind turbines, electric cars, and so on, become more affordable options for the average consumer. As costs drop and they become more accessible to the ordinary consumer, I think the investment opportunities for these assets can produce great returns.

In addition, I do believe moving toward green energy is the ethical thing to do as a society. We must push to use less plastics, as they have been proved to choke off sea animal life in our oceans. There's an epidemic of asthma in children in China due to the high usage of coal in their major cities, which causes air pollution. The effects of the Industrial Revolution and the carbon footprint of mankind are clearly taking a toll on our planet, and the introduction of green energies is vital to remedying the situation.

Mankind has always managed to adapt to continue its growth. Before kerosene lamps, we were killing whales and using their blubber to provide light. This was totally unsustainable and ridiculously backward in retrospect, but we didn't really know any better until we discovered electricity and the lightbulb. Similarly, the United Kingdom once ran primarily on coal. Black lung and other diseases ran rampant in London and other cities in England throughout the nineteenth century. As a result, England moved to cleaner energies and solved their pollution problems. Remember the ozone hole crisis?

Well, we have worked to reduce the production of such pollutants. I find that humans adapt and create new solutions to solve problems such as pollution. For this reason, I am long-term bullish on green energy, not because of some global climate emergency hysteria, but because of the tendency of people to adapt and maintain survival.

ELECTRIC VEHICLES (EVs)

Probably the most prevalent green effort currently is the push to increase the number of EVs on the road. We are seeing nearly every major automobile company creating EV divisions. In addition, certain governments are passing legislation and setting goals for a certain percentage of cars on the road to be electric. Germany, for example, wants to have 1 million EVs on the road by 2030, and the German auto industry is going to invest $45 billion in EVs over the next few decades. However, I do not think that we're all going to move to this utopian world where everyone is driving an EV. This is a fantasy. What many do not realize is that the rare metals needed to build an electric engine and build the batteries that store the energy require massive drilling, leading to serious hurdles production-wise.

A recent study commissioned by Christoph Buchal of the University of Cologne found that the number of resources it would take to mine lithium, cobalt, and other rare earths may pollute more than diesel and gas engines themselves do. There is an ethical dynamic to this equation as well. The great colonial empires were built on exploiting the resources of the colonies (mostly in poor Asian, African, and Caribbean nations) and bringing these resources home to the mother country.

The coffee and sugar of Jamaica, spices from India, and metals from Africa were shipped back to England for the usage of a small percentage of citizens residing in the controlling colony. Exploiting base metals and rare earths in poorer African and South American countries so a bunch of yuppies in San Francisco, Beverly Hills, or New York can drive around in EVs and run their houses on solar seems hypocritical and a form of modern-day colonialism. However, people currently turn a blind eye to this unfortunate situation, because the need for new technology is at such an all-time high. Due to these sustainability concerns, I think we will never go fully electric. However, even if just 20% to 25% of the cars on the road end up becoming electric, there's still a huge opportunity investment-wise.

When investors think of EVs, they think of Tesla (TSLA NASDAQ), as it has been the explosive forerunner in the industry. At this point Tesla is a household name, but just because you are first to the game doesn't mean you will end up winning the championship. In the internet boom, the initial players were AOL and Netscape. In videogames, it was companies like Commodore and Atari. Blackberry, Motorola, Nokia, and Ericsson were some of the first big players in mobile phones.

I believe that Tesla will face a similar outcome in the EV sector. They will act as one of the forerunners, but not a winner in the long term. The big boys such as GM, Ford, Honda, Toyota, BMW, Mercedes, and Jaguar have much deeper pockets than Tesla. Therefore, they can afford to subsidize their losses in their EV divisions with the profits they make in their regular cars. Tesla has no such luxury. On top of this, Tesla has a ridiculous valuation with a market cap over $1 trillion. This is 10 times more than both GM and Ford are worth combined.

It does not seem sustainable. I think that Tesla has serious sustainability troubles down the road, and if there is a downturn in the corporate debt market and economy, they will have issues funding their operations. Tesla could end up being like Blackberry was to cell phones—one of the first to the game, but when the big boys like

Apple and Samsung came to play, Blackberry could not compete. There are also many who question the legitimacy of the accounting at Tesla. For example, they took over their sister company Solar City, which would basically be insolvent right now if not for the Tesla takeover. In addition, China is now the largest producer of EVs and at much lower prices, so low that the United States must put tariffs on China's EVs.

In addition, EVs are proving to be problematic to use on a day-to-day basis. If you want to see some great rants on the problems with EVs, I recommend the YouTube channel The MacMaster (Lee Alexander Davey). It's a food and travel vlog, but Davey owns a Porsche EV and goes on rants about the problems with charging it, the driving range, and so on. It is a great common man day-to-day experience on the problems with EVs.

In addition, many studies have now shown that Tesla EV batteries lose 30% to 40% of their power after just five years. In addition, the resale value of a Tesla now has fallen 50% within just three to four years of purchase. I think all these problems are going to continue, and the EV boom will not be as large as many think. However, there will still be growth and EVs, so let's look at some other companies that produce outside of Tesla.

Competition for Tesla—Vinfast, Rivian, Lucid

It should be noted that 8 of the largest 12 EV companies in the world by market cap are Chinese. They are now the leaders in EVs; this makes sense, as China produces most of the world's lithium, so China produces a large number of EVs.

If you are looking for a conservative investment that is competition for Tesla, you could just buy one of the major automakers: GM, Ford, Toyota, Honda, BMW, or Tata (with Jaguar), all of which are building electric cars.

When doing my research for this book, an interesting company I came across was Vinfast. As you can see from Chapter 5, I am skeptical of Chinese investments; the lack of rule of law, shady accounting, and potential future trade wars have me skeptical. Vinfast is a Vietnamese company. It started to trade in the summer of 2023 and spiked to $90 a share but also quickly collapsed to $4 a share as I write. The company has just over $1 billion in revenues and $9 billion in market cap, so it is still not cheap, but it has doubled revenues in the past two years and is worth looking at. Right now, they are on pace to produce 40,000 cars in 2024; however, their goal is 100,000, and that is about what they need to produce to become profitable.

Rivian (RIVN NASDAQ) and Lucid (LCID NASDAQ) are two U.S. EV automakers. The issue with these other U.S. companies is they have huge valuations and little sales. Rivian, for example, trades at a $15 billion market cap but has a fraction of the sales of GM or Ford, trading at one-third the valuation of each! They did recently see a good-sized investment from Volkswagen, but again it's a long way from being able to be worth $15 billion. It also has a fraction of sales of the just-mentioned Vinfast, which trades at 60% of the valuation of Rivian. Lucid has $6 billion in market cap and about $600 million in revenue. They produce only about 10,000 cars a year. With green subsidies about to disappear under a Republican administration, it hurts these companies, as they are very much in need of them.

RARE EARTH METALS

Rare earths and precious metals are an entire scientific field of their own. To keep the section on rare earths relatively light, we are going to focus on lithium, mainly because it is used globally and is the most well known.

Lithium

Lithium is one of the lightest metals on the earth and is the main component in battery storage technologies. The two main sources of demand for lithium R4 battery storage are for smartphones and green technology, such as solar/wind and car batteries. Smartphone demand should remain stable; however, we are beginning to see saturation in the market. The demand for smartphones will come from replacements as people upgrade and replace phones.

With the expected rise in EV production, we will see an even higher demand for the supply of lithium. Demand for lithium by 2027 is expected to be 1.8 million metric tonnes. The supply by 2027 is expected to be about 1 million tonnes (in 2023, it was only 180,000 metric tonnes!). (See Figure 8.1.) Some of this will be dependent on politics and policies. With Trump winning the 2024 election, we will see all sorts of EV mandates and subsidies disappear. Many of

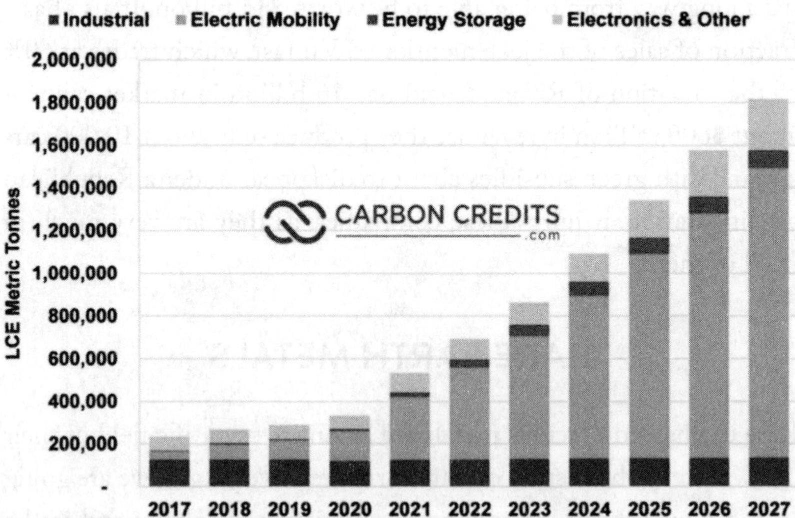

FIGURE 8.1 Is the increased demand for lithium sustainable?
Source: S&P and Bloomberg. Courtesy of https://carboncredits.com/why-lithium-prices-are-plunging-and-what-to-expect/

the lithium and other green equity sectors saw large declines after the election after the Republican clean sweep and Trump victory.

Investments in Lithium

Most of the world's production of rare earths comes from China. With China putting a 25% tariff on rare earth metals in reaction to the U.S. tariffs, you're going to want to look for companies located outside of China. I predict a push for countries to create their own supply of rare earth metals and not be so dependent on China. Currently, the leading producer of lithium outside of China is Australia, producing 50 million metric tonnes of lithium a year.

Lithium had a huge run-up post-Covid trading from 38,000 renminbi in 2020 (this is the Chinese currency, which lithium is priced in globally, as China is the largest producer) to nearly 600,000 renminbi in 2022! It has since collapsed to 100,000 as I write in 2024.

I am active in the junior mining industry. Most of this industry is in Vancouver, and while most in the industry are honest, there are some very shady characters, to say the least. One thing that Vancouver promoters are known for is jumping on the bandwagon of hot sectors. In 1999 when I was starting out in markets, dot-com and tech were the craze, so many Vancouver promoters turned their mining companies into dot-com and tech deals. Then in 2006 uranium was hot, so many Vancouver promoters turned gold and silver mining companies into uranium companies. Then in 2017, crypto and cannabis were the craze, so again they turned gold and silver mining companies into crypto and cannabis deals. All of these time periods basically ended up being the top in those sectors. So in 2020 and 2021 when I saw Vancouver lithium promotions popping up left, right, and center, all I thought was, "Here we go again," and voilà, it ended up being the top in lithium!

With that said, lithium has fallen a great deal, and so some of the larger companies are worth a look at.

The largest producing mine in Australia is the Greenbushes lithium asset, which is operated by Talison Lithium, a subsidiary jointly owned by miners Tianqi Lithium (SZSE:002466) and Albemarle (ALB NYSE). Greenbushes is the longest continuously operating mining area in Western Australia, having been in operation for over 25 years. Albemarle trades on the NYSE. The stock has also fallen 70% from its all-time high, falling from $300 a share in 2021 to roughly $109 at the present.

The second-largest global producer of lithium is Chile, producing over 16 million tonnes a year. Chile's largest producer is Sociedad Química y Minera de Chile S.A. (SQM NYSE). Like Albemarle, this company had a large run-up into 2021 and has fallen a great deal from a high of nearly $100 a share to $38. The company also pays an impressive dividend yield of near 5%.

There is also a lithium ETF, the Global X Lithium & Battery Tech ETF (LIT NYSE), if an investor wants diversified exposure to the sector. This ETF went up nearly six times in price from 2016 to early 2021 and has taken back just over half those gains since 2021. Lithium stocks have fallen, but I do not think we are at the point of maximum pessimism yet. I feel maximum pessimism is when assets fall 75% to 90% in price or more, and lithium is not quite there; however, if it were to fall more, I think some of the investments I have outlined are worth looking at.

Zinc Ion as a Potential Alternative to Lithium

One option to replace lithium batteries for grid-scale storage is the zinc-ion battery. Zinc-based batteries are generally less expensive than lithium-based batteries, as zinc is a more abundant and less expensive material than lithium. This is a recent technology that has only been around for about 10 years or so. They have less storage capacity and provide less energy than lithium, which is the problem.

They are also much safer and have much cheaper material costs and easier recycling options.

There are very few zinc battery companies. I recently invested in a micro cap in Canada that has been working for years in zinc battery technology. This company is too small to mention in these pages and is a turn-around play.

I should note this is a risk in many of these new "green tech" companies. So much money is being thrown around at them from the government level; yet many of these companies are just garbage companies that are looking for government handouts, so you must look diligently at those that are real. It has been estimated that nearly $1 trillion in market cap has been lost in green tech companies since 2021.

Another reason I believe zinc batteries will be promoted is China produces most of the world's lithium. Since zinc is much more abundant than lithium (about 100 times more zinc is mined a year than lithium), it will reduce reliance on China if zinc batteries can become economical for energy storage.

A Zinc Battery Play: Eos Energy Corp Inc. (EOSE NASDAQ)

A company that trades and produces zinc ion batteries is Eos Energy Corp Inc. (EOSE NASDAQ). The company trades around $4 and has a market cap just north of $900 million (I initially recommended EOSE in *Financial Intelligence Report* at $1 a share). They are in the initial stages of their production and storage technology and only have about $17 million in revenue. This stock was trading at $28 a share with a market cap in the billions at the top of the market bubble in 2021.

According to the *MIT Technology Review:* "Eos's batteries use a water-based electrolyte (the liquid that moves charge around in a battery) instead of organic solvent, which makes them more stable and means they won't catch fire, Richey [vice president of research and development at Eos] says. The company's batteries are also designed to have a longer lifetime than lithium-ion cells—about 20 years as opposed to 10 to 15—and don't require as many safety measures, like active temperature control."*

The company recently received a loan from the DOE and is hoping to store enough battery power to power over 100,000 homes in Pennsylvania by the end of 2026.

As we go to press, the company has announced some impressive news. On December 18, 2024, they announced a 400-MWh stand-alone storage order with International Electric Power (IEP). As noted in *Yahoo! Finance*:

> This marks the second agreement and third project with IEP, a leading developer in the energy space deploying multiple technologies, and builds on Eos' successful prior delivery of its battery systems to a Texas-based IEP project earlier this year.
>
> The project, partially funded by the California Energy Commission's (CEC) Long Duration Energy Storage Program, is set to be deployed at Marine Corps Base Camp Pendleton in San Diego County with expected delivery to begin in 2025. This order, which is structured with a down payment, represents a significant milestone in the continued commitment to enhance grid resiliency and advance sustainable energy solutions within California.†

This has the potential be a huge company going forward in the energy storage arena.

---

*Source: https://www.technologyreview.com/2023/09/06/1079123/zinc-batteries-boost-eos/.

†Source: https://finance.yahoo.com/news/eos-energy-secures-400-mwh-133000572.html.

Cobalt

Another high-demand precious metal is cobalt. Cobalt is used in alloys for aircraft engine parts and in alloys with corrosion-/wear-resistant uses. These properties make it widely used in batteries and in electroplating. Cobalt salts are used to impart blue and green colors in glass and ceramics. Radioactive 60Co is used in the treatment of cancer. Cobalt is also used in samarium-cobalt permanent magnets, used in guitar pickups and high-speed motors. Cobalt has a wide array of uses in many technological fields, and its rising demand is met with an interesting hurdle. It is very difficult to find pure cobalt companies, as most cobalt is produced as an offshoot of copper or nickel production.

Glencore (GLNCY Pink Sheets)—the Largest Cobalt Producer

The largest cobalt producer in the world is a conglomerate, Glencore, which produces 27,000 pounds of cobalt a year. This is about 60% more than the runner-up in production, making Glencore a dominant player in the cobalt sector. Glencore is a unique resource company in that it is not just purely a producer; the company also trades commodities. It's based in Baar, Switzerland, a sleepy town of 21,000 people. During the cheap money boom in commodities from the early 2000s into 2011, Glencore leveraged itself and took over numerous mining assets. They were then hit hard due to this leverage in 2015 when commodity prices fell hard. However, the company has restructured and is now much leaner.

Currently, Glencore trades at $9 a share. During its plunge in 2015, it fell from $8 to $1.50 a share; in 2020 it again fell from $8 to $2. As Glencore has a history of boom and bust, I wouldn't be buying Glencore here, but if you want a cobalt play for the long-term demand in batteries, it's worth a mention. I would look at Glencore if it were again to fall below $6. In addition, if you agree with our thesis on the coming to "QE for the people," Glencore is a solid way to play that, as it produces all sorts of metals from all over the world.

Company Vale do Rio Dolce (VALE NYSE)–Iron Ore with a Cobalt Kicker

The other company with cobalt exposure we will discuss is Vale, a Brazilian producer of iron ore also responsible for a large amount of cobalt production. When iron ore prices tanked a few years ago, this company was hit hard, but it has since recovered. The company, which peaked at $18 a share in 2011, fell to $1 in 2015! It has since rebounded to $11. Vale is more of an iron ore play; however, in the longer term, if cobalt prices rise due to the demand from electric vehicles, it may trade more in the price of cobalt.

NUCLEAR: THE FORGOTTEN CLEAN ENERGY

The green movement is ignoring nuclear power. There is a bright future and great opportunity in it. Nuclear already plays a large role in global energy production. Nuclear power provides over 10% of the world's electricity and 18% of electricity in Organisation for Economic Co-operation and Development (OECD) countries.

The demand for power will grow even more, with nuclear power production estimated to grow by 46% by 2040—more than 90% of the net increase will come from China and India, according to the International Energy Agency (IEA). In 2017, China added three nuclear reactors to its production, bringing its total in operation to 41.

While some have mixed feelings about the safety and sustainability of nuclear power, its efficiency and production capabilities are undeniable. Investing in an established nuclear company as opposed to an upcoming alternative energy company is also an idea worth exploring.

Électricité de France SA (EDF.PARIS, ECIFY Pink Sheets)

Over 80% of France's power production is nuclear. The French aren't exactly what we would generally regard as "far right" politically, so it shows that if you put your biases aside, you can provide a cheap, plentiful source of power.

Due to its expertise in running France's nuclear power industry, Électricité has gotten interest from India in the development and operation of its new nuclear facilities. The company has a contract to build six of India's nuclear plants. On top of nuclear, the company is diversified in wind and solar as well. Currently, the company's roughly €71 billion in revenue is made up of 64% of nuclear power and 8% of renewables such as solar and wind.

The company is also a solid dividend play, paying a dividend of over 1.5%, making Électricité a definite name to look out for.

Uranium

The easiest way to invest in the growth of demand for nuclear energy is uranium. There are a few companies that specialize in producing nuclear energy, whereas there are many companies that produce uranium. Uranium in its pure form cannot be used for energy production; it is the process of turning uranium into plutonium that makes it ready for production (and radioactive). This is what makes it crucial in the process of nuclear energy production.

Uranium demand, which is currently near 175 million pounds a year, will rise to nearly 250 pounds over the next 10 years. The price of uranium saw a huge move from $10 to $140 per pound from 2000 to 2006; it then crashed to under $20 but has since rebounded to as high as $100 again in 2024. (See Figure 8.2.)

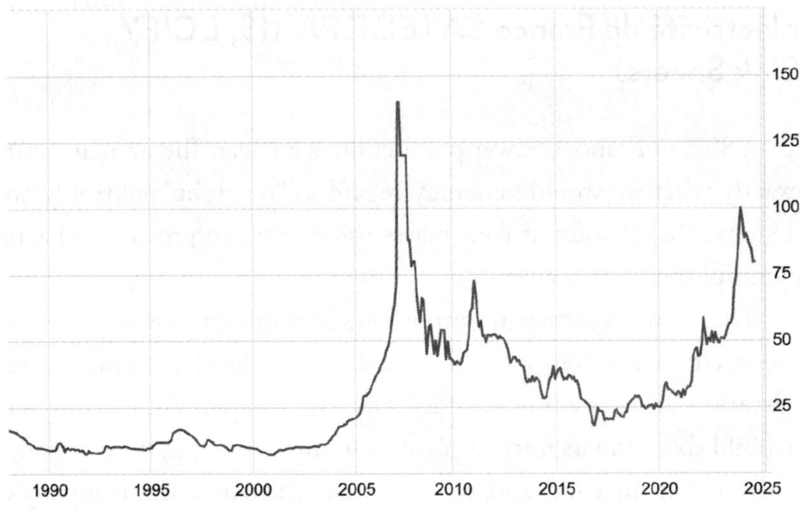

FIGURE 8.2 Uranium price.
Source: www.tradingeconomics.com

Uranium Stocks—What Do They Have in Common with Dot-Coms and Other Bubbles?

When we think of bubbles, we think of booming economies, new technologies, and growth industries. American stocks in the 1920s, Japanese stocks in the 1980s, dot-coms in the 1990s, and the recent crypto currency bubble all come to mind. However, a smaller and more recent boom and bubble was experienced in uranium stocks during 2002 to 2007. At that time uranium was coming out of a 20-year bear market, and all sorts of announcements were made public about new Chinese nuclear reactors coming online. This fed the fuel to the fire of a uranium bubble. Many uranium stocks became the "hot thing" in mining and soared in price. Many uranium companies blew off in 2006, after rising hundreds of percent in price, then crashing 80% or 90% or even more since. The silver lining here is a nearly 13-year bear market has created some notable value in many of the companies in the sector.

Another interesting potential driving factor for nuclear energy is it could be an energy demand play on artificial intelligence (AI). AI needs a ton of energy to produce, and many companies in the AI sector are asking for more production of energy to educate the supply and demand for AI. Recently, it was announced that the infamous Three Mile Island nuclear plant that nearly melted down will be reopened with its sole role being production of energy for AI. AI is similar to the dot-coms or telcos of the late 1990s bubble in that even if the price of the AI equities is a bubble, the long-term demand will be huge and the reopening of nuclear plants and demand for uranium may be a way to invest in the long-term AI boom!

Uranium Stocks

Most uranium stocks are very small producers or junior mining companies. Cameco (CCJ NYSE) is the one large-cap producer, with a market cap of over $4.2 billion. During the bubble in the 2000s, Cameco went from a historical low of $2 a share to $50 a share. It then fell below $10 a share as uranium busted in the 2010s. It then rallied back strong as uranium prices surged back to $100 and is trading around $40 a share as I write.

When you have a huge bust and bubble like this, it is hard to know when the stocks will move again. For example, after the tech bubble burst, Amazon fell from $110 to $5 a share from 1999 to 2001, and after the 2009 bear market and financial crisis, Amazon was still only $35 a share! It wasn't until 2010 that Amazon finally, 11 years later, surpassed its 1999 highs. Many tech stocks took even longer to break their tech bubble highs. For example, it took Microsoft nearly 15 years to take out its 2000 highs. Will Cameco, like Amazon, Microsoft, and Apple, surge past its previous highs and soar? Only time will tell. Like them, it took over a decade to get back to its highs and now it is sitting around them. If you are just looking for one uranium stock, in my opinion, this is the one.

If you want to diversify your uranium investments, try the Global X Uranium ETF (URA NYSE). This is a diversified ETF that holds companies with uranium production. This ETF was over $90 at the peak of the commodities bubble in 2011 and now trades at only $30!

SOLAR AND WIND POWER

These are the two most popular forms of energy for those promoting the Green New Deal and green economy. The reason is once they are in production, they produce no greenhouse gases, making them extremely sustainable environmentally speaking. However, they are currently nowhere near the most affordable of alternative energies. Hopefully, as the technology behind solar and wind continues to develop and introductory costs drop, solar and wind should be able to compete with natural gas and other cheap forms of energy and electricity. (See Table 8.1.)

In addition, Figure 8.3 shows the cost of solar per megawatt since 1977.

TABLE 8.1 The cost of wind and solar compared to other energies in terms of setting up the electric grid

Energy Plant Type	Lifetime Cost $ per MWh
Offshore Wind	138.0
Coal with 30% CCS	130.1
Coal with 90% CCS	119.1
Biomass	95.3
Advanced Nuclear	92.6
Nat Gas Combined Cycle with CCS	74.9
PV SOLAR	63.2
Hydroelectric	61.7
Land-Based Wind	59.1
Natural Gas Combined Cycle	50.1
Geothermal	44.6

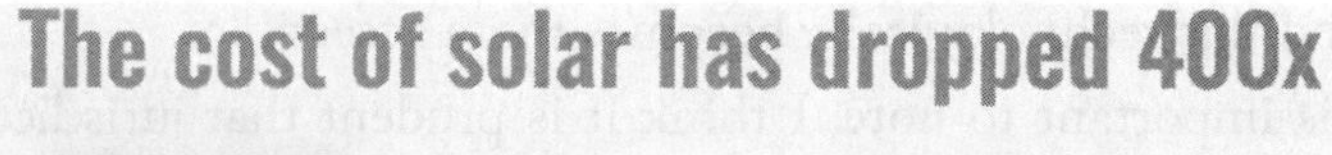

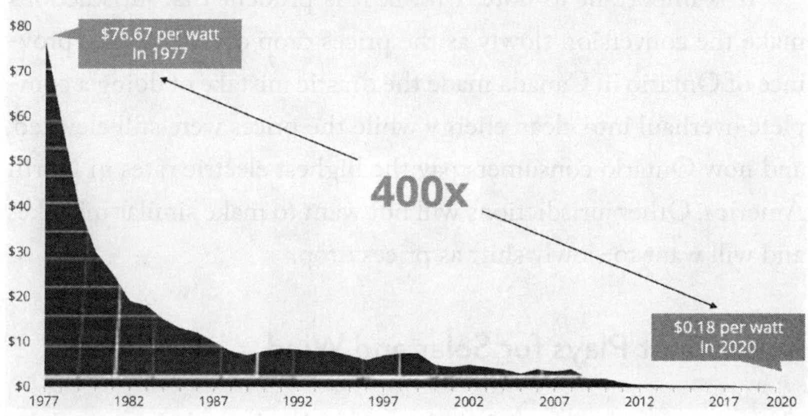

FIGURE 8.3 Price history of cost of solar per megawatt.
Source: https://www.freeingenergy.com/facts/cost-solar-has-dropped-dramatically-g116/

The cost of solar installation has fallen over 99% in price from $77 per watt in 1977 to roughly $0.18 per watt in the past few decades. We must remember this is the cost of installation so this $0.18 is on top of the added costs. Solar is still about 30% more expensive than natural gas (the cheapest form of energy production), but it is definitely getting more competitive.

It should also be noted that these costs are the costs in the United States (which has some of the cheapest electric generation in the world). I reside in the Bahamas, which uses diesel electrical plants, and costs are astronomically high, in some cases four times what they are in the United States. Therefore, in the Bahamas solar and wind are much more economical to install. Many European countries, such as Germany, are moving toward more solar and wind power and away from carbon fuels. Germany is expecting to have over 50% of its energy be produced from renewables by 2040. Many more jurisdictions will slowly implement renewables as the costs drop and this technologically becomes more accessible.

It is important to note, I think it is prudent that jurisdictions make the conversion slowly as the prices drop over time. The province of Ontario in Canada made the drastic mistake of doing a complete overhaul into clean energy while the prices were still elevated, and now Ontario consumers pay the highest electric rates in North America. Other jurisdictions will not want to make similar mistakes and will want to slowly shift as prices drop.

Investment Plays for Solar and Wind

The easiest way to invest in solar would be through Invesco Solar ETF (TAN NYSE). TAN is off nearly 90% from its 2008 highs of $240, trading near $26 a share. It has a market cap of over $300 million and holds companies such as First Solar, SolarEdge, and Sunrun.

First Solar (FSLR NASDAQ)

The largest of the solar companies in terms of market cap is First Solar, which has north of $3.5 billion in revenues. Back in 2008 solar was one of the bubble sectors along with housing. Part of the reason was the huge run-up in oil prices at the time. Often when oil and gas experience a spike in value, it makes solar options more alluring, so they often catch a bid as investors and consumers look for alternatives to high energy prices. When there was a huge run-up in oil to nearly $140 a barrel in 2008, solar equities increased along with the oil price. At that time First Solar soared to over $300 a share! However, by 2012 First Solar had sunk to nearly $20 a share. It has since rebounded and now trades at roughly $190 a share. Since falling more than 90% in price, First Solar has rallied nearly 1,000% in price! First Solar was whacked after the election with the fear that solar and green subsidies would decline, but it is still the leader in solar power.

Canadian Solar (CSIQ NASDAQ) and SolarWinds (SWI NYSE)

While First Solar is arguably the largest and most well known of the solar companies, that does not mean it's the cheapest. Canadian Solar is a formidable company, and my views on that are not biased from being Canadian. The company's financials and valuation are much better than First Solar's. The company has a puny $1 billion market cap despite that it has over $7 billion in revenues and trades at five times earnings! In addition, while First Solar has soared, Canadian Solar has fallen from $50 a share to $12 a share since 2020. Canadian Solar looks like an excellent long-term buy-and-hold value plan in the solar sector.

If you want a smaller company, SolarWinds has almost doubled its revenues from $428 million in 2014 to $766 million in 2024, and like Canadian Solar, it is trading well off its 2020 highs.

Wind Stocks

In the wind sector, the main ETF is First Trust Global Wind Energy ETF (FAN NYSE). It is much smaller than the solar ETF, but yields a nice 1.7% dividend. One of the largest wind companies in the world is Vestas (VWDRY pink sheets), which trades on the Copenhagen exchange. This is a Danish corporation, which is the leader in building wind fields and plants in Europe, which is one of the fastest-growing markets for wind power. Both are great potential investments, and if you're looking in the wind sector, start here.

CONCLUSION

I do not feel there's any truly clean energy. Virtually anything needs some form of natural resources. The plastics essential to solar panels are derived from oil and gas. Building windmills takes a ton of steel and other resources. The batteries in energy storage come from lithium, cobalt, and other metals. The American election result in 2024 will hurt short-term demand for these metals in the United States. However, the rest of the world will continue moving toward energies that use less fossil fuels in their output. In this chapter, I have outlined nearly all the potential investments to profit from this environmental trend.

Conclusion

One thing I've learned in my nearly 30 years in the markets is whether it be in investing or in politics, don't believe the most extreme views. Doom and gloom sells but does not always come to fruition. You also must be a realist, and the fact of the matter is this bull market is long in the tooth and valuations are extremely stretched in U.S. equity markets. In addition, the bubble has been driven by excess loads of debt and cheap money. The Covid crash in the spring of 2020 was a warning of things to come. There are opportunities in a crisis.

This book explains the risks from these bubbles and how to profit from their potential bursting. However, it also gives opportunities that exist in the investment world. If I'm correct, you do not want to be invested in the sectors that have benefited from the recent debt and asset bubbles. You do want to invest in the sectors that are benefiting from new technology and the shift from the hypernormalization of the everything bubble to a focus on the real economy via what I call "QE for the people."

This book also preaches patience. Many of the investments I outline are not yet at the levels I would like to see before investing aggressively. However, it's always good to have something on your radar screen. It's like shopping for a big screen TV. You may see one you like but not want to pay the outrageous price it has when it's first released. However, if you see that same TV on sale, at some point it becomes a good value, and you save yourself a lot of money in the meantime before the purchase.

I don't mean this book to be an investment bible or the be-all and end-all of investing. I think if it just opens people's eyes to new opportunities rather than chasing "hot sectors," it has served its purpose.

The market is a massive "bubble." When the market "tops out" as it did in 2000, 2007, and 2020, it obviously becomes extremely vulnerable to any external shocks. We are coming to the end of an era—the era of massive equity bubbles. This has continually picked up steam and accelerated since the 2008 financial crisis. Since the United States got off the gold standard in 1971, we have seen an explosion of debt at all levels of the global economy. From government debt, consumer debt, investment corporate debt, junk corporate debt, student debt, to emerging market debt, the list goes on. When the global economy went pure fiat in 1971, it meant that nothing backed the fiat dollars and other currencies in circulation, so governments could de facto print as much money as they wanted.

Back in the 1980s, there was a period of financial liberalization: Ronald Reagan, Margaret Thatcher, and other leaders deregulated financial markets. This, combined with a pure fiat system, became a perfect scenario for the financial markets. The financialization of New York and London, along with currencies that could be printed limitlessly, resulted in great prosperity in the financial and credit markets.

For the past 15 years, the explosion of debt and ease of money printing has caused global stock market and property market expansion. However, it has also left governments worldwide vulnerable to a large downturn in the economy. The result of these bailouts is grim;

the impending downturn will inevitably bankrupt affluent Western nations and send shockwaves through second-tier economies.

I firmly believe we are nearing the endgame of this debt super cycle, and the Coronavirus Crash was the catalyst for the impending transition as the money printing and spending that happened after 2020 ended the near 40-year bull market in the bond market.

Since 2009, we have seen a gross acceleration of the debt bubble. During the worst periods of the 2008 financial crisis, governments saw an explosion in deficit spending to keep economies afloat, and in many cases they had to rack up enormous deficits to bail out the financial system.

Take Canada, for example, a nation that had a debt-to-GDP ratio of about 70% before the 2008 financial crisis. Canada's debt-to-GDP ratio is now near 100%. The increase of debt is not unique to the government's deficit. In fact, a similar trend can be seen across many different sectors. Student loans in the United States, estimated at roughly $650 billion before the financial crisis, have now surpassed a figure of $2 trillion! Furthermore, corporations have nearly tripled their debt in the last 20 years from $3 trillion to $10 trillion—a figure that comprises nearly 40% of GDP. Keep in mind, much of this corporate debt was incurred by funding buybacks and keeping the stock market bubble afloat.

The biggest issue with all these staggering numbers is very simple. The room for growth is limited. Before the current financial crisis, many governments had low debt-to-GDP levels after a near-20-year global economic expansion. However, these debts accrued as governments ran huge deficits to keep economies afloat during the financial crisis. Subsequently, the failure to balance budgets and pay back debts during the time of economic upturn has led to massive increases in debts and leverage for many large corporations and governments alike.

Nowhere is this more apparent than in the United States, the global superpower and largest economy in the world, where nearly 10 years into an economic expansion, deficits were running over $1 trillion (nearly 5% of GDP prior to 2020). In 2024 as I write, the United States is again going to run a near $2 trillion deficit, or nearly 7% of GDP, and this is during an economic expansion!

The danger is that there is no cushion for debt to continue to accrue in the future; there is a limit. The government will not be able to stimulate or absorb the downturn after another market crash on par with 2008. If there is any sort of return to the "bond vigilantes" (investors who will crush bonds and raise longer-term interest rates, looking for larger returns or forcing governments to become financially solvent), then governments will be broken at every major international level.

The government bailed out the financial sector during the last two financial recessions, but who will bail out the government? We already witnessed this from 2010 to 2012, as the so-called PIIGS countries (Portugal, Ireland, Italy, Greece, and Spain) saw interest rates spike when their debts went out of control following the recession. This debt crisis was controlled by the European Central Bank (ECB). However, I am primarily concerned with the impending scenario where superpowers such as China and the United States will need to be bailed out or print money to bail themselves out.

Will DOGE be successful in cutting government spending (which will still cause short-term pain) but avoid a longer-term debt crisis? Only time will tell.

This book is not doom and gloom. While the current state of the global economy is indeed alarming, you must not let the failure of large governments and multinational corporations to properly manage their funds negatively affect your investment decisions. In fact, quite the opposite—with the bursting of the bubble, great opportunities will arise for the informed investor. The world financial system is experiencing serious changes in terms of emerging technologies, fluctuating commodities and precious metals markets, and debt-servicing capabilities.

Even the fiat system is evolving with the developments and implementation of cryptocurrencies globally. With so many rapidly emerging and changing markets and sectors of the economy, many opportunities will present themselves for financial gain in the short and long term alike. The future may seem bleak to some, but remember it is always darkest before the dawn and the best time to buy is at the point of maximum pessimism. So keep your chin up and your outlook bright, and let's make some money from times when things look the bleakest!

Index

Page numbers followed by *f* refer to figures.

About the Author

DAVID SKARICA is the founder and editor of *Profit From Pessimism*, which uses the contrarian investment techniques outlined in this book to buy value assets and prosper from them overshooting to the downside. He is also the editor of *DollarHedge Insider* and was the founder and editor of *Addicted to Profits*, a popular and influential newsletter and website known for its stellar performance in both up and down markets from 1998 to 2023. Addicted to Profits is still a consulting company which helps with expats moving offshore.

Skarica entered the financial markets at the preciocious age of 18, and became the youngest person on record to pass the Canadian Securities Course. He is a regular speaker at trade and investment conferences and has been a regular guest on the Business News Network (BNN), Canada's flagship business broadcasting network. The author of six books, Skarica's first book, *Stock Market Panic! How to Prosper in the Coming Crash* published in 1998, predicted the bear market in U.S. stocks from 2000 to 2002 and boom in gold, silver, and other commodities in the coming decade. And his third book, *The Great Super Cycle: Profit From the Coming Inflation Tidal Wave and Dollar Devaluation* published in 2010, predicted that years of huge debt and government spending and money printing would lead to huge inflation and a bust in the bond market from 2021 to 2023.

Skarica's work has appeared in publications such as *Newsmax*, the *Bull and Bear Financial Report*, *Barron's*, *Investor's Digest of Canada*, and *Canadian MoneySaver*. He finished second in the

Globe and Mail's stock picking contest in 2003. That same year stockfocus.com ranked his former service, *Addicted to Profits*, the fifth-best-performing newsletter out of 300 newsletters! Skarica also has edited *Gold Stock Adviser* and *Gold Stock Advisor Pro*, and has contributed to *The Financial Intelligence Report*, published by Newsmax, since 2009.

Skarica is a huge fan of the English football team Leeds Utd and the American football team Las Vegas Raiders. He writes *Raider Greats* (www.raidergreats.com) as a fun side venture and is also a huge fan of the Canadian show *Trailer Park Boys* and the '80s TV show *Miami Vice*. He loves old-school rock 'n roll music, with his favorite artists being Robert Palmer, the Power Station, ACDC, and INXS. And in 2020, he was featured in the Wonton Don series, *Donnie Bahamas: Corona Refugee*, on Barstool Sports.

He resides in Eleuthera, Bahamas, in a hilltop house 150 feet above sea level, where he watches the sun rise and set with his cat, Peanut, aka "The Big Sheriff."

Visit the author at:

www.ProfitFromPessimism.com

https://www.youtube.com/@profitpess

https://www.patreon.com/c/profitpess

https://profitfrompess.substack.com/

www.DollarHedgeInsider.com